HOW TO
ENJOY YOUR CHILDREN
and
HAVE AN EASY LIFE

Janet <u>Monica</u> Head

SRN (Eng); SCM (Scot); QUIDNS (Scot); RSI (HV Cert. RNC Lond); NSCN (Eng).

EDWARD GASKELL
DEVON

First published in 1999 by
EDWARD GASKELL *publishers*
Unit 7
Caddsdown Business Park
Bideford
Devon EX39 2EA

isbn 1 898546 - 33 -9

HOW TO

ENJOY YOUR CHILDREN

and

HAVE AN EASY LIFE

Janet Monica Head

SRN (Eng); SCM (Scot); QUIDNS (Scot); RSI (HV Cert. RNC Lond); NSCN (Eng).

Printed and bound in the EC by
The Lazarus Press
Unit 7 Caddsdown Business Park
Bideford
Devon EX39 3DX

DEDICATION
to the mothers who requested that I write this book –
it would never have been written otherwise

ACKNOWLEDGEMENT

To Ann C. Tilbury
who so patiently edited and word-processed this book

CONTENTS

CONTENTS (Continued)

CONTENTS (Continued)

CONTENTS (Continued)

CONTENTS (Continued)

CONTENTS (Continued)

Edward Gaskell *publishers*

FOREWORD

I met Monica Head as the friend of a friend. I do remember her saying she had written a book and was having difficulty in getting it typed up. I do not remember how or why I agreed to take on this task for her.

I have never read any serious childcare books. Only the little paperbacks which one is recommended to read when pregnant, and the various near-leaflet books given away at ante-natal classes and in maternity hospitals.

I was very impressed by the book. It is full of good sense. Good "old-fashioned" sense. And it is so easy to use with short non-waffling chapters.

So many mothers these days do not have their own mothers around to hand out advice. Either because they have moved far from their roots or because they are having their children late in life, as did I, when their own mothers have died.

She writes like a member of the family which so many mothers do not have; a cross between mother, grandmother and nanny. You can almost hear her brogue coming through the print, and she is a very plain speaker, writing in capital letters and with much use of exclamation points to underline until one can nearly hear her firm but kind voice.

When I showed her current newspaper cuttings relating to various subjects covered in her book we discovered that she had covered each of them, and in great depth.

Monica calls on over 50 years of experience to write this book. Memories of the "Real Depression" are relevant today. She tells her readers how to "feather your own nest and not that of the companies". She comes up with basic ideas which will give the modern woman cause to think; when did someone last seriously suggest you tethered your child? When did someone give detailed instruction on discipline? Follow her guidelines for feeding and you will have a non-crying baby. No more stressed mothers.

I feel this book can be summed up in three words: basic common sense. But never has such a book been produced before, and even the format of the book is one of basic common sense.

Monica is to childcare what Margaret Powell was to housekeeping.

I most unreservedly recommend you to read this book!

Ann C. Tilbury

HOW TO
ENJOY YOUR CHILDREN
and
HAVE AN EASY LIFE

1

INTRODUCTION

This book has been written in accordance with its title – *How To Enjoy Your Children and Have An Easy Life.* You may never before have heard or read the advice which follows. A short history of my career might help to explain the reasons for the advice given.

I was trained as a Nanny in a private residential nursery in the slums of Liverpool. Life was very austere; no domestic staff and rigid discipline. We had the children for twenty four hours a day except one half day per month. This meant that each nurse had six babies from two weeks to six months old, or six baby-toddlers from six to eighteen months old, or six toddlers from eighteen months to five years old, SLEEPING WITH HER IN THE SAME ROOM, every night. Should a child wake during the night I need not spell out what happened to those looking after them (one's sleep was not made up!)

Employment as a private Nanny demanded the children must be good sleepers during the night and contented during the day. Child Welfare Clinics were not attended by this social class. Unsolved difficulties were referred to the G.P. – entailing doctor's fees. Too many of those, and one's employment was terminated; possibly without a reference.

Later I became a State Registered Nurse, a midwife and a Queen's District Nurse, working in many parts of the Highlands and Islands of Scotland, sometimes with no available doctor. Any child repeatedly awake at night; I was called out, battling with 100 mph gales, to the far flung crofts with no road to them. Not being keen on this part of the work I made sure the advice given kept the children asleep at night and I – in my bed!

For many years I have worked as a Health Visitor and continued to give the advice contained in this book. Providing the child is not handicapped it should not fail – but instructions must be carried out.

As a young mum said: 'This book is like any unusual recipe; unless all the ingredients are used and the instructions followed exactly, one cannot be disappointed if it does not turn out!'

It is at the request of many mothers that I have written this book. I have endeavoured to write the instructions in a simple manner. Do not forget; I am only human! In some parts perhaps I have failed to make myself clear, or failed to include a subject on which you hoped for advice. Should you fail to get the results required, PLEASE contact me, via my publishers' address on page ii. State your problem clearly and enclose a stamped self-addressed envelope and I shall be more than pleased to reply.

After all, this book has been written to help parents and those in charge of children.

2

YOUR HEALTH VISITOR

1. She is a trained Nurse.
2. She has Midwifery experience – some are fully trained Midwives.
3. She is trained to deal with Medical and Social problems.
4. Health Visitors have held responsible posts in hospitals.
5. She may also have various other Nursing qualifications.

Your Health Visitor is a very qualified person in both Medical and Social work. In fact she is a medical-social worker; responsible for all from the ante-natal mother and father to the oldest inhabitant in the area. In other words she is involved from the cradle to the grave and adept at everything between unblocking the kitchen sink to giving some legal advice.

The major difference between your Health Visitor and a Social Worker is that the former has in some instances five to six nursing qualifications. She is capable of spotting the medical condition which so often triggers a social problem. Really she is your best friend; do confide in her. Given the chance she may work wonders.

Have confidence in your H.V. – she always has time! Like the policeman, she may not be on the spot when needed but they both can always be contacted.

Many problems may loom up. To you it is "Just one of those things" which one has to put up with. But why? If not discussed it may develop into a real problem in years to come.

But how does your H.V. know that YOU need her? – She is not inspired! PLEASE phone her even though you feel whatever you wish to discuss is trivial. Leave her to be the judge and allay your fears. Failing to contact your H.V. may result in her making ten visits in one morning but only seeing three families. A thorough waste of time when others require help and advice. THIS IS WHY THERE ARE HEALTH VISITORS.

WHEN YOU ARE PREGNANT

1. Decide whether you would prefer a hospital or a home confinement.
2. The National Health Service pays Maternity Benefit.
3. The Health Visitor or Midwife will advise regarding benefits.
4. Mothercraft Classes are arranged at Health Authority clinics or at the hospital where you attend for ante-natal appointments.

The majority of expectant mothers book for a hospital confinement without even considering the advantages of having their baby at home. Once a mother has experienced a home confinement she is surprised to discover just how wonderful it can be. Your own things around; not to mention your family. Loneliness is not one of the worries during labour; you are the only concern of your midwife.

One mother stated: "I shall never go into hospital again unless I have to."

"Why did you go?" I asked.

"We are brainwashed. We are not given the option."

Should any complication occur during a home confinement a special Maternity Ambulance with all emergency equipment is ready to transfer you to hospital.

Some G.Ps do not wish to undertake Domiciliary Midwifery. Under these circumstances it is in order to procure the services of a G.P. who is prepared to accept you during the ante-natal period and confinement. This is a temporary arrangement only.

Mothercraft Classes are held for your benefit. Should you also wish to attend before your second baby is born you may do so.

4

SOME REASONS FOR DRINKING STOUT

1.   Take stout at least for three months without fail after confinement.
2.   ALL the time while breast feeding and three months AFTERWARDS without fail.
3.   If you have older children and you have not taken stout before add on three months for each child.
4.   Looking after elderly/sick relatives whether living with you or living in their own home: It is IMPERATIVE you drink stout daily.
5.   Running your own home and going out to work.
6.   Tension at work (both sexes). Stout daily.
7.   Recovering from debilitating disease/illness such as flu or depression.

Some of the reasons for taking stout I have endeavoured to list in chronological order. Should you be one of the "Unfortunates" on sedatives TAKE HEED. Replace the sedatives with stout but do ask for medical advice. The alternative is to remain on sedatives, eventually becoming addicted and possibly remaining on sedatives for the rest of your life.

Reading this sounds like a commercial — Stout is the cure for ALL ills. Well, it is, more or less! Think for a minute. How many everyday illnesses, including nervous breakdowns and so on, are initially caused by stress, strain, sleeplessness, (inability to fall asleep) and insomnia (waking in the early hours), plus ineffective sedatives?

Stout is a very strong beer – hence the sedative action. It is also full of iron. Perhaps now you can realise why the Irish labourers of the 1800s and early 1900s were capable of such continuous navvy work – digging canals, sewers, making and repairing roads – all done by pick and shovel. Surely this is enough to convince anyone of the benefits of stout, which they consumed frequently.

Throughout this book I have endeavoured to solve the problems of early childhood – but parents' problems require solving also. It is no good having good children while the parents are nervous wrecks incapable of enjoying their own lives or those of their children.

Of course there are some parents who revel, (if that is the right word) in being martyrs to the cause. "But my child...." etc. "The doctor said...." etc.etc. "He's had all the tests...." etc.etc. And so they go on. This is heard in surgeries, clinics, on public transport, everywhere. Mother and child subjects dominate all conversation.

I have spent hours, when I was Health Visiting, trying to persuade these *martyrs to the cause* mothers to follow my advice but to no avail. Their unfortunate husbands are always greeted – on their return from work – with lurid, weepy, descriptions of the day's problems.

To these mothers I say – neither myself nor anyone else can be of assistance. These mothers can only press on regardless – suffer! They make sure they do not suffer in silence. No wonder many of their marriages end in divorce. In later life they are the ones who invariably have menopausal problems.

5

HOW AND WHEN TO TAKE STOUT

1. A small can before retiring to bed.
2. Early Evening.
3. Diluted: Ice Cream Soda
             Fizzy lemonade
             Sweet Cider   Sufficient to make
             Port   the drink palatable
             Milk
             Soda Water

"It is heavy." "It is bitter." "I can't stand beer." And, of course, "I forgot." "It puts on weight!" How many other excuses expectant mothers, and the mothers suffering from nervous exhaustion make! I leave it to you to add to the objections.

The first objection I mentioned, "It is heavy" — Of course it is heavy, otherwise it would be no good at all! It gives the relaxation required instead of sedatives. To avoid the weight problem adjust your intake of calories, especially luxuries.

The usual amount is a small can each night before bedtime. This normally results in a deep relaxed sleep, so much so that you may waken with a fuzzy head in the morning. DO NOT BE ALARMED. Two headache tablets will soon rid you of that: It is similar to having a long lie-in which can result in a headache. The blood pressure is lowered because of deep relaxation. The following night take the drink earlier in the evening. Remain in you own chair. When you feel drowsy DO NOT RETIRE TO BED OR LIE DOWN ON THE SETTEE. Place a pillow behind your head, make yourself comfortable and sleep. One mother jokingly said "Sleep off the hangover!"

If, on the other hand, the small can has little or no effect on you, it means you are in a state! A large can each night is then required and taken until you are sleeping properly in approximately two to three weeks. After that time reduce the stout to one small can.

Take it EVERY NIGHT WITHOUT FAIL until the time comes when you waken at about 3.00 am full of the joys, and with enough energy to move house! You have now reached the stage when stout acts as a stimulant instead of a sedative. Drink it during the day in your "Flagging Period"

Again I can hear the cry " I can't stand beer at any price; not even the smell!" SO WHAT? Surely you have taken things you disliked before this? Ever thought of diluting it? Dilute to your own taste but you MUST, MUST, MUST drink the can of stout, in spite of the quantity of flavourings.

Do not worry should you require to get up during the night to spend a penny. You will drop off to sleep again without trouble. As you become used to the flavour of the stout you will more than likely decrease the quantity of the additives.

Believe me – after a fortnight I could tell you whether you have taken it daily or not! It makes all the difference. Eventually you will be able to do without it.

§

6

WHEN TO CONSULT YOUR GP RE TAKING STOUT

1.   When prescribed certain drugs.
2.   Certain medical conditions such as diabetes and others.
3.   Alcoholism or drug addiction.
4.   High blood pressure.

There are several drugs in this day and age which prohibit the taking of alcohol under any circumstances, especially when driving.

A number of medical conditions, which I am unable to list here, do exist as contra-indications to alcohol. The majority of folk who regularly attend their G.P. have a good idea of the reason for their treatment. Where necessary the G.P. states "No Alcohol" when handing over the prescription.

On the other hand, some doctors just do not approve of stout at any price. When you ask permission they just raise their eyebrows, shrug their shoulders and say it is a waste of money, TAKE IT AS READ that you are at liberty to drink it.

ADVICE NOT USUALLY GIVEN

7

ELASTIC STOCKINGS

1. As soon as you realise you are pregnant purchase, or through the NHS prescription, two pairs of elastic stockings.
2. Have them fitted by an expert.
3. Wear them all through your pregnancy and one month after confinement.
4. Any social occasion when wearing short dresses use elastic stockings.
5. This is a sure way of preventing varicose veins.

The wearing of elastic stockings is probably far from the minds of young pregnant mothers especially when looking at the glamorous pictures and posters of the pregnant mothers so familiar to us all.

I cannot stress too strongly the importance of elastic stockings worn EVERY DAY throughout pregnancy. Lighter ones may be worn when attending a social function. Remember! the lighter the stocking, the less support it gives.

Put on the stockings BEFORE RISING in the morning and certainly BEFORE the foot has gone over the side of the bed. This prevents discomfort later in the day when the stockings can feel too tight.

When changing to the lighter stockings have the feet on the bed. Remove the elastic stockings and then put on the lighter ones in the same operation.

As a rule stockings are not prescribed until varicose veins appear. This is too late; irreparable damage has been done.

Take my advice; wear stockings. It is better to be safe than sorry!

VARICOSE VEINS

1. The increasing weight of the baby in the womb impedes the return of the blood from the legs.
2. Once veins are varicosed there is no real cure.
3. When treated other veins must carry a heavier burden.
4. The consistent wearing of elastic stockings throughout pregnancy is the best safe-guard.

There is nothing more devastating to elegance than varicose veins. Yet how many mothers-to-be are prepared to run the risk of developing such veins and, what is more, to do nothing at all to prevent this dreadful condition.

Not only can they not be cured, they cause pain, discomfort and possibly varicose ulcers in later life. When out shopping observe the knotted veins accompanied by the heavy walk of the older woman. The foot and the ankle lack movement, also notice the young woman pushing a pram; attractive hair-do, smart clothes but not always smart legs because of varicose veins.

Approximately 90% of varicose veins can be prevented by supporting the legs with elastic stockings during the day and the use of lighter ones when the occasion demands.

Support stockings are a must from the third month of pregnancy until a month after the baby's birth. It is VERY IMPORTANT that they are put on BEFORE RISING IN THE MORNING WHILE YOUR LEGS ARE STILL ON THE BED.

Varicose veins may, on the surface, appear to improve after confinement but you are unable to see the deep-seated veins which are weakened and varicosed.

Veins can be treated but the treatment means the remaining veins have extra work to do; a case of whipping a tired horse. To PREVENT re-occurrence after treatment, and I am talking about possibly years later, it is ESSENTIAL TO WEAR SUPPORT STOCKINGS FOR LIFE if you have not followed my instructions.

9

CRAMP

1. This is almost the commonest cause of lack of sleep.
2. Lack of water is the usual cause.
3. Lack of calcium, salt or both.
4. Take calcium lactate during pregnancy (on prescription).
5. Pressure of the baby: use pillows for support in bed or when resting on a settee.

Cramp is very painful as those who have experienced it know. Although so common very little has been done about it. The usual causes are lack of water, pressure of the baby, lack of calcium or lack of salt.

We live in a very affluent society. As a nation we are over-fed, under-exercised and overdosed. OUR BODIES SUFFER FROM A MAJOR DEFICIENCY; WATER! Few drink an adequate quantity, not because of scarcity, but there are more interesting things to drink. Tea coffee, squashes and so on do not count as water. They are classed as fluids.

WATER IS A NECESSITY. The kidneys eliminate waste products according to the amount of water in the body. The remainder are retained, result; cramp – in later life arthritis.

Athletes, especially on a very hot day, can suffer with cramp. Running and jumping demand excessive expenditure of energy, ABNORMAL perspiration and so reducing the water and salt content of the body. The waste products due to exercise are retained by the body causing cramp.

A pregnant mother does not take violent exercise but her kidneys must cope with the waste products of herself and the baby. Cramp is insidious. It does not happen overnight. It can be cured in three days providing that *half* a glass of water is drunk EVERY HOUR of the day while she is out of bed. The result is not drastic! One does not "Disappear" every five minutes! Water taken in small quantities at frequent intervals is retained in the blood stream and the body tissues.

The weight of the baby may cause pressure on a nerve. This is more difficult to cure or relieve. A good maternity corset is essential. Ensure the support is from the lower abdomen upwards. When in bed: (1) Use a small pillow in the small of the back crossways. (2) Lie on one side with a pillow lengthways down the back. turn onto the back until the pillow acts as a support. (3) Place a pillow crossways under the knees. One or more of these suggestions may have the desired result.

Lack of calcium can cause pains in the legs. This is a sign of the baby absorbing calcium from the mother at her expense. For extra calcium consult your G.P.

Lack of salt due to excessive perspiration is rare in this country.

§

10

SLEEP

1. The absence of cramp and other discomfort.
2. To ensure sleep, especially after confinement, take a small can of stout immediately before retiring to bed.
   CHECK with your G.P.
3. The sleep routine is usually broken in the later months of pregnancy
4. Remember your Relaxation Exercises (No 11) and put them to practical use.

Reasons other than cramp are capable of preventing sleep. The main causes are tension due to familial worries, finance, housing and so on, or just being "Under the Weather". Those who do not "Get Going" until mid-morning and/or feel over-tired in the evenings are included in the "Under the Weather" class.

In spite of having eight hours sleep at night very few are fortunate to have eight hours of complete relaxation. This is proved by so many nervous breakdowns, (puerperal depression), and difficulties with sexual marital relations, especially after having two or three children.

To attain the happy state of "Feeling Alive" first consult your doctor. A mother may be a diabetic or be taking prescribed drugs which ban alcohol. With your doctor's approval take a small can of stout before retiring to bed. This is a great relaxer: less harmful and MORE EFFECTIVE THAN SEDATIVES. Take the stout after confinement and continue three months after you discontinue breast feeding or three months after confinement if artificial feeding is adopted. There is nothing in the world will do what stout does. It is an acquired taste. Fizzy lemonade, ice cream soda, tonic water, cider or lager may be added to the small can. Any one of these additions can make it palatable.

During the months of pregnancy, retire to bed early. This allows time to lie awake quietly or carry out the relaxation exercises until sleep takes over. DO NOT make the mistake of making a cup of tea. Tea is a stimulant and also the very fact of getting out of bed wakens you up.

§

11

RELAXATION EXERCISES

1. Stretch hard the muscles of your feet; hold and relax.
2. Add to those the muscles up to the knee, including the feet.
3. Add to those the remaining muscles of the whole leg.
4. Stretch muscles of the hands; hold and relax.
5. Add to the hands the muscles to the elbow.
6. Add the muscles of the whole arm; hold and relax.
7. Screw up the face tightly; hold, relax.
8. Repeat with all the muscles involved.
9. Repeat No 8 as often as necessary.

IMPORTANT

During these exercises breath in deeply and out slowly. It is surprising how soon you will start yawning. Apply the pillows as described in Cramp (No 9).

12

BREASTS

1. Some women continue to menstruate during the first three months of pregnancy.
2. The breasts start to tingle.
3. The nipples change colour and the base covers a larger area.
4. At three months a few drops of colostrum (milky fluid) can be squeezed out.
5. Massage the breasts daily with castor oil or baby oil.
6. Always use a good supporting bra.

Commence early in the pregnancy to massage the breasts with castor or baby oil to prevent stretch marks appearing which will later spoil the contour of the breasts. Continue this at least until you have finished breast feeding; by which time you will have found how good the oil is for your skin and be using it all over regularly!

Wear a good supporting bra all through pregnancy and through the night when sleeping. Do not leave breasts unsupported when feeding the baby. The breast used for feeding, support with the hand, the other leave in the supporting bra until required.

Unsupported breasts stretch the muscles and full breasts are heavy.

13

PREPARATION OF NIPPLES

1. Carry out advice from the BEGINNING of pregnancy DAILY or more often if possible.
2. Whether you intend to breast feed or not – carry out the advice.
3. Purchase the softest toothbrush available; a child's, for example.
4. Mix methylated spirits and olive oil, in equal parts, to half fill a bottle (to allow for shaking – emulsifying).
5. Use the toothbrush at least DAILY to scrub the nipples.
6. AFTERWARDS use the methylated spirits and oil.
7. Shake to emulsify.
8 With thumb and first finger roll the nipples using the mixture.
9. At the same time pull the nipple from the breast.
10. At the same time support the breast.
11. THIS APPLIES WHETHER, AT THE TIME, YOU INTEND TO BREAST FEED OR NOT.

I am not condemning the mother who does not wish to breast feed her baby but you have at least six months during which to change your mind one hundred times or more. The answer is to be prepared! Should you not breast feed, nothing is lost, but if after the babe is born and you wish to change your mind, your nipples are ready, and this is all that matters. Many mothers abandon breast feeding because of inadequate preparation. Those pregnant with their baby usually work to the seventh month and not until then are they free to attend Mothercraft Classes. During Mothercraft Classes you are instructed what to do but at six or seven months the advice is often too late for breast feeding.

The treatment is very simple but often the simple is the most difficult to put into practice, especially if you have no intention of breast feeding. Discipline yourself!

Many mothers have said "If only I had the advice earlier I could have managed!" This is tragic for both mother and baby!

A home confinement means the Midwife has time and patience to help you during the ante-natal period and afterwards. In hospital, due to numbers, individual encouragement is sometimes absent and so many babies are artificially fed, in spite of the mother desperately hoping to feed her babe.

Again, I repeat, should you not breast feed your baby, whatsoever the reason, DO NOT FEEL GUILTY.

§

14

STRETCH MARKS (STRIAE GRAVIDARUM)

1. These are ugly.
2. They may fade in time.
3. They cannot be effaced.
4. Castor or baby oil massaged into the abdomen daily can usually prevent them.

These marks on the abdomen, similar to those on the breasts, are caused by the muscles tearing as they become overstretched to accommodate the growing baby. They are very unsightly and certainly not becoming when wearing a bikini. They also slacken the muscles permanently.

Massaging castor or baby oil into the abdomen can either prevent these marks or reduce them considerably but the treatment must be carried out daily to keep the skin and muscles supple.

Like varicose veins, once they appear there is no cure! The remedy is in your hands. begin the treatment during the early months of pregnancy.

ANTE-NATAL REQUIREMENTS

15

THE MOTHER

1. The Midwife will provide a list of articles required.
2. A breast exhaust is more than useful; it may prove rather diffi cult to obtain in this modern age. Order one in advance.
3. A man's pyjama jacket is more useful than a night dress during labour, especially during a home confinement.
4. A co-operative husband and family.

The Midwife will give you a list of articles required; usually for a hospital delivery. The pyjama jacket is not required for a hospital delivery. Gowns with back openings are used. For a home confinement which, I feel, may become fashionable before long, a pyjama jacket really is a must. It saves the mother having a soaking wet nightdress removed from over her head after her waters break, so keeping her hair clean. The mothers agreed the pyjama jacket worn back to front and buttoned at the back proved more comfortable, it remained dry during confinement and was so easily removed.

A breast exhaust is a very useful item of equipment. It looks rather like an old-fashioned motor horn with a small reservoir for the milk. The exhaust does not empty the breast; ONLY the baby can do that. Should the breast become too full it is useful to draw off the surplus milk. It is a MUST if you wish to lead a social life. Refer to Breast Feeding (Nos 33-37)

Avoid the danger of being too proud to accept help and suggestions from your husband and family.

Involve the toddlers and older children. An excellent way is to make your own baby clothes. Use a simple magyer pattern using attractive or plain material. The toddlers will be interested. the older children could tack the garments together ready for you to machine.

16

THE HUSBAND

1. Be present at the birth; the baby is a joint affair.
2. Get your wife to describe and demonstrate to you what she has been taught at ante-natal classes.
3. Help and encourage your wife during the exercises.
4. Some clinics hold an evening ante-natal session for the benefit of both parents.
5. Take the opportunity to "Bath the Baby" – the life-size demonstration doll.

Request your wife to demonstrate to you what she has been taught at each session of the ante-natal classes, especially the ante-natal exercises. There are leaflets and books on the subject supplied by the clinic. Read them and learn them. Then you are able to conduct these exercises. The regular exercises and the time spent doing them is more interesting when you both work together.

Some clinics hold an evening session for the benefit of both parents. Take the opportunity of "Bathing the Baby". The baby being a life-sized doll.

As the pregnancy progresses life becomes more difficult for your wife. Sleep becomes more disturbed as time goes on. At the end she is carrying around approximately 10 lbs (4.5 kgs) of flesh and blood (including placenta and liquor). Quite some feat!!! If in doubt hang 10 lbs of potatoes around your waist and see how you manage!!! Due to lack to sleep she may be tired and irritable. She may not know what she does want. This is where your patience and kindness come in.

Personally I feel it imperative husbands are present at the birth – be it spontaneous, forceps or caesarean. Your wife cannot walk out, why should you? This means you become totally involved.

17

THE BABY

1. The layette. Preferably cotton in Summer.
2. Vaseline. Necessary when changing the nappy.
3. Talcum powder. Can manage without.
4. A good supply of nappies.
5. Expensive items are not necessary.

One mother said to me "A baby is as expensive as you care to make it." Not a truer word was spoken!

The most important article is a good supply of nappies. More essential than ever should the family be living in an awkward bed-sit. the washing of them is reasonably easy but drying is the problem. A 10 lb load of nappies can be taken down to the launderette, washed and dried without wasting money. A launderette drier helps avoid the necessity for wet nappies to be draped around a bed-sit. Do not think all this is a waste of money. Later the nappies, with very little trouble, can be made into pants which are easily washed and require no ironing. Of course very popular today are the disposable nappies but, from a personal point of view, I feel they are VERY expensive considering their limited use and price continually rising. Before finally deciding to use them compare the price of one dozen turkish towel nappies (which you can make yourself) against the cost of disposables for approximately 18 months. So long as water remains on water rates and not metered I think you will find turkish towelling nappies cheaper. When away from home, camping or caravanning disposables are ideal.

Should money be scarce, in the case of very young married couples, magyer dresses, rompers and nightdresses can easily be made. No sewing skill is required and they are easily ironed. This makes life easier by cutting down ironing time, saving electricity and giving more freedom.

Plain, unscented soap can be used both for washing the baby's head as well as his body and an unscented talc is cheaper than the fragrant variety but not substandard – but if the babe is thoroughly dried it is not necessary. If you must use talcum powder sprinkle a LITTLE on your hand or fingers and SMOOTH it into the armpits, the groin and under the chin.

Do not forget, a baby is as expensive as you make it!!! Do consider Thrift Shops! The result is the same. Use the extra money to feather your own nest and not the nest of the manufacturers.

IMMEDIATELY AFTER THE BABY IS BORN

18

THE MOTHER

1. Give the mother a good cup of tea or coffee.
2. Should she wish for a good meal give her one.
3. Perhaps the labour has been long and trying. She may be tired. Allow her to sleep first before seeing the baby; that is if she prefers things this way.

The mother is thirsty and quite likely to be hungry. After a cup of tea some mothers would appreciate a meal of bacon and egg or some other form of substantial food. When I was practicing Domiciliary Midwifery one hungry mother was tucking into a bacon sandwich while I was delivering the after-birth. "Terrible!" I can hear many say, but "Thank you very much" says the hungry mum with her troubles over.

§

19

THE BABY

1. Give the baby a good drink of plain boiled, cooled water even before a feed or before bathing.
2. Once the clearing up is done the baby may have two or four minutes at the breast or a drink of whey.
3. Increase time gradually until full breast feed is taken. See Clock Feeding (No 46)

The baby is often very thirsty after birth. When bathed give a good drink of plain boiled, cooled water (SMALL-HOLED TEAT ESSENTIAL). Afterwards either put the baby to the breast or give a drink of whey (again, small-holed teat), if the mother is too tired after a forceps delivery or a long and difficult labour; which can be the case in a home confinement in remote rural areas wherever they may be. This depends on the particular midwife in attendance. It was a practice I always carried out under abnormal circumstances. Whey is the nearest approach to colostrum and can be made during labour according to instructions on the rennet bottle. For an artificially fed baby who has had a bad forceps delivery this is excellent.

The whey, like the colostrum, does not need digesting only absorbing, enabling the digestive organs to gradually become accustomed to digesting milk.

Colostrum also acts as an apperient to rid the bowel of meconeum (which acts as a lubricant to the bowel), resulting in a black stool. As the meconeum is finally passed the colour of the stools changes to that of freshly-mixed mustard.

§

20

THE TODDLER AND OTHER CHILDREN

1. In the case of a home confinement settle the mother and bath the babe.
2. Bring the toddler into the room and sit him on the floor with his back to the wall and a very firm pillow under his arm.
3. Place the baby into his arms.
4. Leave him to nurse his baby while the clearing up is done.
5. NEVER put the toddler with a baby on a bed or a chair etc.
6. Give the toddler the baby to nurse each time the babe is out of the cot or pram, placing the pillow under his arm.
7. If a hospital confinement, greet the toddler on your return home. He has already met the baby in hospital.
8. Give the baby to the toddler to nurse AND THEN GO out of the room to remove your coat – providing there is an adult present.
9. Of course he will be sitting on the floor.

HOME CONFINEMENT. After the mother is settled and the baby bathed, sit the eldest, (regardless of age), ON THE FLOOR. Support the back against the wall or stable furniture. Place a firm pillow under the arm and give each child in turn the baby to hold. During this time the clearing up is done, while an unsuspected eye is kept on the enraptured youngster. None of these children will harm the baby. Please, would-be-critical adults, leave the toddler alone to get on with the job of nursing the baby and getting to know him.

HOSPITAL CONFINEMENT. In the case of a hospital confinement the mother, on her return, should greet the toddler then give him the baby to nurse BEFORE removing her coat.

When the toddler has been staying with relatives, try to arrange his return just before a feed. Change the baby and hand him over to the toddler.

In time he will get used to the baby and his hand will start wandering. His fingers will travel towards the eyes. When the eye lashes are touched the finger is poised so delicately while the baby's eye closes. None of his toys have spontaneous movement and this is the object of the exercise! DO NOT WORRY. A baby will never suffer in silence. So long as the baby is quiet the toddler (11 months upwards) is doing no harm.

Toddlers of 11 to 12 months old are not really capable of holding a baby on their knee. Place a pillow on the floor. Sit the toddler down with his arm on the pillow. Lay baby down with toddler's arm under the baby's head. Two to three minutes may be sufficient. Be guided by the toddler. It is strongly advisable to remain in the room but do not intervene unless the baby cries.

Always allow time for the toddlers and school children to nurse the baby whenever he is out of the cot. This rules out jealousy. it also prevents young children throwing toys into the pram for the baby and trying to feed him while in the pram. Both are dangerous practices. Apart from this the mother is in peace to feed her baby during which time she can have a rest. One mother invariably sat in a rocking chair while feeding – proving most relaxing for both mother and babe.

I repeat, DO NOT allow a child to nurse the baby when sitting on a chair or bed. If so a parent must not leave the toddler alone. This means the baby belongs to the mother and the poor toddler is only "Being Allowed..." Think how we would feel if someone gave us something precious to hold, then kept breathing down our necks in case we dropped it. There is no need to print what one's reaction would be. The same applies to the toddler; LEAVE HIM ALONE. The reward is absolute. the look of ecstacy on his face is a 'joy to behold' – as one mother described it.

§

21

THE HUSBAND

1. I hope you husbands have helped your wives during their pregnancy!
2. After the babe arrives there is extra work.
3. There are both pleasant and not so pleasant duties to perform, for instance changing and washing nappies.
4. With the first baby your wife, like yourself, wears an L plate.
5. Do not allow your wife to be over-possessive of the baby.
6. You must be prepared to give up some outdoor pleasures. Your wife needs companionship. She does not expect to become a Pub or Golf Widow.
7. Remember the baby has two parents. Not one plus a financial provider.

This is one of the most important chapters of the book. No doubt you have already read the notes on The Husband (No16).

Some husbands at first feel they do not wish to be present at the birth of their baby, but to give a few words of encouragement and help with relaxation during his wife's labour pains will mean so much to her. After all, your wife cannot opt out, no matter how long or difficult the labour may be.

Many happy marriages totter and may, in time, finally break after the arrival of the first baby. A mum can be so "knowing" that her poor husband finds it impossible to cope with an over-tired, over-competent mother who has become a *Martyr to the Cause*! Do not allow your wife to act like this. The babe is also yours!

Work is also increased in every respect after the birth. This ought to be shared. It is good to adopt the idea that when one sits down, both sit! As the family increases this applies even more! Work shared means the husband giving up his regular outings with "The Boys". A considerate husband will automatically do this. I go so far as to say it is his duty! To achieve this is sometimes difficult: The wife goes out shopping, the husband thoroughly cleans the bedrooms; walking through the door, the wife sees the living room in the same state as before – "Why waste time with that when there is all this to do!" He cannot win! The beginning of her becoming a Pub or Golf Widow! He goes out with The Boys: "It does not matter what I do, I can't win. To save rows I leave her to get on in her own time." In the first place your wife ought never to be allowed to reach this condition. This is the one reason why I have written this book in such detail. Follow ALL the instructions, NOT just those that suit you! And don't forget her stout!

Demand to bath your baby as soon as you have him to yourselves. As one dad said to his wife, "I'll bath the baby, my hands are bigger than yours, you may drop him."

From then on the children have two full-time parents to help and guide them through childhood and the stormy teenage period. There is more about this later in the book.

CRIES OF A BABY

1. THIRST
2. TOO HOT
3. COLD
4. HYPOTHERMIA
5. OVER-FEEDING
6. UNDER-FEEDING
7. WIND
8. COLIC
9. DISCOMFORT
10. HUNGER
11. LONELINESS

§

22

HOW TO DETECT THIRST

1. A baby cries between 6.00 pm and 10.00 pm because of thirst and NOT HUNGER as commonly thought.
2. Within two days of birth a baby is capable of drinking 3 ounces (9.0 cl) of boiled water at one time.
3. Water, (without sugar) should not be rationed.
4. A small-holed teat MUST BE USED.
5. Refer to How to Cut Out Night Feeding (No 47) and two hourly routine – Clock Feeding (No 46)

This is a situation seldom appreciated during the early days of life. Milk at the best of times is a thirsty drink because of the high sugar content especially when sweetened for babies.

Water, as a drink (no sugar) is the only fluid that quenches thirst. Orange juice, sweet vitamin drinks and so on contain sugar and ultimately increase thirst.

Water should NEVER be rationed. Providing the baby is offered it at regular intervals the daily intake will vary according to surrounding temperature, age and size of baby.

Do not be surprised at the quantity of water a baby drinks. Just think how deprived he would be if it were not offered. He would cry.

When the baby refuses water while crying vigorously with a "Coughing" cry, check the teat. A medium-holed teat allows the water to come through too quickly and chokes the baby. Hence the resistance.

Always presume thirst before hunger otherwise the baby will have an excessive weight gain because he is trying to quench his thirst on milk alone.

One or two breast fed babies may cause concern because of persistent refusal of a bottle of water. Use a spoon. The water is not the cause of the trouble but a too-fast teat. Using a small-holed, (slow), teat offer a drink before and after each feed and in a day or two the teat will be accepted.

Depending on the method of sterilisation it is a good idea to rinse the bottle and teat with boiled water. Sterilising fluid flavours water. The flavour may render the drinking water unacceptable to the baby.

If short of water while crossing a desert, and then having a choice of drink, it would certainly not be orange juice or anything similar but water! We cannot do without it.

Water to a baby feels different to milk! He will very soon become used to it. It is nature's way of protecting the baby. In bygone days there was not always pure clean water available.

When four to six weeks old, offer water BETWEEN FEEDS. Waken the baby two hours after food; for example 10.00 am feed, mid-day water and so on throughout the day. Within two days the babe will waken for water as regularly as he does for food. You can then change the nappy, give a drink of water and "Pot" the baby. He will probably use the pot 5-10 minutes after feeding or drinking, so the Mums tell me. Discomfort, thirst and a change of position – three reasons for a baby crying – scotched at one go.

23

TOO HOT

1. The baby will cry.
2. The hair is wet around the ears and perhaps around the neck line.
3. A pram with the hood up is one of the main causes, especially when standing in the sun.
4. Over clothed or using nylon during very hot weather.
5. THE BABY QUIETENS WHEN PICKED UP AND HE COOLS DOWN.
6. Give a long cool drink of unsweetened boiled water.
7. Use the shade of the house to cool the baby down.
8. Move the pram with the sun.
9. Do not put the hood up.

Naturally the baby cries and the hair round the ears is wet and also, possibly round the neckline. This is the only way one is sure of arriving at the correct conclusion.

NEVER leave the babe lying in direct sunlight without canopy or shade and NEVER with the hood up. The temperature inside that hood can rise to the same temperature as that in a car standing in the sun all day: up to 130 degrees F. Put your head under the hood and find out for yourself.

Use the shade of the house or of a tree should a canopy not be available. A rotary clothes drier covered with a sheet is excellent. Move the pram around with the sun if using the house for shade.

A hot baby is very thirsty. A long drink of plain boiled water is called for (and only water). Wind the baby during the drink, giving a short rest then more water if required. See Winding (No 51).

24

COLD

1. The baby cries vigorously.
2. THE CRYING CONTINUES EVEN AFTER BEING PICKED UP.
3. The crying continues until the baby is warmed by the mother's body.
4. The baby is quiet while being fed.
5. While winding the crying will start again.
6. The process is continued.
7. The feet are VERY cold to touch.
8. Should there be any doubt, make the baby too hot, then strip off as necessary.
9. If the baby is outside in the pram in cold weather, it is ESSENTIAL THAT A THOROUGHLY WARMED SHAWL, wrapped round a HOT water bottle, is taken outside to the baby.
10. Turn back the pram covers, cover the baby with the shawl and pick up the baby.
11. Place the hot bottle in the pram and replace the covers.
12. Remove the bottle when the baby is put back.
13. This also applies should the cot be in an unheated room.
14. The baby seldom cries when put back into a warm cot or pram but will always do so if the cot or pram is cold. He continues to cry until it warms up.

This condition is more common in babies and young children than some people realise. Every other reason is given instead of cold, because the condition is so difficult to detect.

COLD IS THE FORERUNNER OF HYPOTHERMIA (low body heat). That is a subnormal temperature. The condition is very serious and can result in death but more about that later.

The most vulnerable period is between early Autumn and late Spring, especially during the damp or wet weather.

IF IN DOUBT presume the baby is cold. Add extra garments and extra covers to the pram until the baby is too hot. Then pick the babe up and allow the pram/cot to cool, then commence to remove a garment or cover – repeat until the required heat is arrived at. That means a quiet baby. EXTRA COVERS must be added both ABOVE AND BELOW the mattress and tucked well in all round, especially if using a wicker or open-sided cot.

When the baby is out in the garden in the pram ALWAYS have his FEET into the oncoming wind. The wind blows over the covers and over the baby's face. This is good for the baby. The other way is the baby with its HEAD to the oncoming wind. This is bad. The wind blows down into the blankets, Result, freezing cold pram and a cold baby.

Baby-toddlers and toddlers suffer in the same way. They are generally miserable with a bright red tip to their nose.

To convince mothers that their babies are cold is a mammoth task. Because the mothers are not cold themselves they fail to appreciate that their children may be. In one morning's visiting I found three cold babies. One mother said she was horrified that only after putting extra clothing on her child did she realise how cold the poor thing must have been. The red nose and miserable crying had disappeared.

25

HYPOTHERMIA

1. This condition is ALWAYS proceeded by cold.
2. The baby is lethargic (sleepy).
3. A cold baby cries vigorously, a hypothermic babe does not necessarily do so or may have a weak cry.
4. The babe has a "Red-Button" nose.
5. Red-blue swollen hands, very cold to touch.
6. Exceptionally ruddy cheeks.
7. Cold feet.
8. Subnormal temperature.
9. If this condition is not treated it can result in DEATH.

I do not wish to frighten you but I must stress this serious condition.

Providing you follow IMPLICITLY the instructions on Cold (No. 24), you have nothing to fear.

Should there be any doubt, EVERY Health Visitor and Midwife has a special thermometer and on request will be only too pleased to take your baby's temperature for you. This will verify the condition without any shadow of doubt and they will give the necessary instructions to rectify this threatening condition.

Remember, Health Visitors/Midwives are unable to live on your doorstep but they can always be contacted, so there is no excuse.

The signs and symptoms are opposite to cold. The baby has gone past the cold stage; he is half frozen. The condition is not so prevalent in centrally heated homes, except during power cuts, but mothers must be on the alert where there is no central heating.

The main thing to remember is: IF IN THE SLIGHTEST DOUBT, ASK.

OVER-FEEDING

1. The majority of babies are over-fed, this is one of the main causes of crying.
2. The SCREAMING starts any time from 7.00 pm onwards INTO the night, and even until 5.30 am. In other words turning night into day.
3. The baby will miss the 6.00 am, possibly the 10.00 am feed also, or he may be drowsy.
4. Drinks of water do not relieve the screaming.
5. This programme is repeated every night.
6. BREAST FED BABIES CAN ALSO BE OVER-FED.
7. The babe will take more food, as sucking temporarily relieves the pain, but screaming starts again.
8. There is excessive weight gain.
9. There is chronic constipation.
10. Gripe water becomes the "Daily Food".
11. The excuse is, "He is a very hungry baby".
12. Instead of being hungry, the poor little thing is CRIPPLED with pain because of too much food.
13. Read ALL my instructions on feeding (Nos 34-59).
14. Could lead to over-eating in later life.

The majority of babies are over-fed due to too thick a mixture of powdered or tinned milk. These babies are seldom given water to drink to quench their thirst. The excuse is, "He is a hungry baby". This results in the giving of solids at a very early age which disguises the over-feeding because the baby is taking less milk.

The so-called "Hungry" baby (depending on the degree of over-feeding) suffers from colic. The result is the poor unfortunate is stuffed with more food, including solids, at too early an age. This may stop the baby crying as much because the solids prevent the infant taking an excessive amount of wrongly measured dried milk or too much breast milk.

The excessive weight gain rules out hunger. The typical over-feeding pattern is "Turning night into day". Crying commences anytime after 6.00 pm and CONTINUES INTO the night until all hours. A thirsty babe ceases to cry after 10.00 pm feed.

The pain of over-feeding is equivalent to the abdominal pain when an adult suffers from "The Bug" (diarrhoea and vomiting).

Now that mothers realise this I hope they will be more sympathetic and not shrug it off with the all too familiar phrase "It is three-month colic!"

Providing all feeding instructions are adhered too, this condition will not occur.

NB. DO NOT OVERLOOK THAT THIS IS A CAUSE OF BATTERED BABIES.

§

27

UNDER-FEEDING

1. The baby wakens about half an hour before feeds.
2. The babe, in spite of everything, CRIES OUT OF THE NIGHT.
3. The babe sleeps after food but has not had sufficient to last until the next feed.
4. The baby generally cries and is miserable and restless.
5. He does not scream or pull his legs up as in over-feeding.
6. The crying is not spasmodic.
7. Constipation may be present but the stools are scanty and green. DO NOT confuse with gastro-enteritis which is quite different.
8. Weight gain is continuously low. See Weight Gain (No 39).
9. Under-feeding can apply to both breast and artificially fed babies.
10. Cracked nipples.
11. Pink's Disease. See Pink's Disease (No 60).
12. Engorged breasts.

Under-feeding against over-feeding is the lesser of the two evils. With the under-fed baby one can do something about it, more or less immediately. In over-feeding, too much food is given, there is nothing to relieve the pain, it has to run its course.

An under-fed baby is generally miserable and the screaming for two hours after food, as in colic, is absent. After feeds the baby settles but has not sufficient food to carry him through to the next feed – hence the crying. If water is given regularly, thirst can be ruled out.

Constipation may be present because the lack of food prevents the stimulation of the bowels. This means stools are scanty and may be green but DO NOT confuse these green stools with gastro-enteritis! Gastro-enteritis stools are frequent and contain mucous (slime), and smell foul!

The weight remains stationary or there is a very low increase approximately a CONSTANT 1-2 oz (28-57gms) weekly gain.

Follow the instructions on feeding and Clock Feeding (No 46) carefully in order to rule out under-feeding.

§

28

WIND

1. Getting breast milk too quickly. Give about 1 oz (3.0 cls) of water before a feed to slow the babe down. Failing that a nipple shield is useful. This is a glass dome to which is attached a small-holed teat. The dome fits over the nipple and acts as a reservoir for the milk and the baby can take the milk at his own speed through the small-holed teat.
2. Giving correctly measured food too quickly. A SMALL-HOLED TEAT is essential.
3. Giving incorrectly measured food.
4. Giving too much food without winding; breast or bottle.
5. Crying starts half an hour to one hour after food.

This is more easily coped with than other major feeding problems. Seldom these days is a mother left during the early days without help from her husband or a relative. During this period the mother can devote her time to the baby.

Winding a baby is like filling a rubber hot water bottle: Too much water poured in at once results in the air being retained or the air pops out throwing the water before it.

BOTTLE FEEDING. It is essential that the food is measured correctly and a SMALL-holed teat is used.

It is necessary to alter the rhythm. Instead of winding once halfway through the feed and then at the end, do so after every half or one ounce (1.5 or 3.0cls) of food and be patient. This takes approximately two days. While altering the rhythm the feed may take one hour. After two days the baby will pop up the wind immediately after each half or one ounce and the feeding is completed in 30-35 minutes.

At first the babe will yell but do not worry. The crying will decrease until, after two days, there is no crying. Also there is no possetting (vomiting) of food.

BREAST FEEDING. When the breasts are full there is great pressure behind the milk. The flow varies, depending on the power of sucking and size of the milk ducts.

Three quarters of the feed is taken during the first five minutes. The pressure is reduced in those first five to six minutes and becomes normal.

The baby requires winding after every half minute for the first five minutes. Take full advantage of help available and in two days the feed will be completed 30-35 minutes (including twenty minutes sucking plus winding).

Should there be difficulty, give the babe approximately one ounce (3.0 cls) of water before each feed, to take the edge off the baby's appetite.

COLIC

1.   This is about the worst pain a baby can suffer.
2.   The pain of over-feeding is one and the same, only colic is more intense and of longer duration.
3.   Colic is purely WRONG FEEDING and NOTHING ELSE.
4.   Over-fed babies ALWAYS have colic.
5.   A baby with colic always has wind.
6.   Colic rears its head two hours after food.
7.   Again the gripe water bottle is well to the fore.
8.   Again the condition is usually diagnosed as hunger.
9.   The baby may quieten, taking cereal, but this is not the cure.
10. The cereals take the place of milk. This does not alter the fact that the milk food is either incorrectly measured or is incorrect ly given.
11. Gripe water can help and even quieten the baby but making medicine the daily food is wrong and VERY WRONG!!!
12. Carefully read my directions on the measuring and the giving of food (Nos 41 &42).

This condition is passed off with a shrug of the shoulders with the excuses "It is three-month colic" or "A baby who requires very little sleep". All very profound, but not much help to the poor mother who has to put up with her poor distressed baby.

Colic is simply indigestion due to wrong feeding. Not until the food has passed the stomach and has been absorbed from the intestines is this dreadful pain relieved. Until this stage is reached the poor baby suffers – and how it suffers!

Gripe water becomes the daily food! It contains a curative indigestion substance, also an aperient, for the obvious reasons, (constipation) but usually with little effect.

Colic is simply wrong feeding. A simple cause with devastating results for the baby and mother. Follow the instructions regarding the measuring of food. One cannot afford to be careless – EVER. If you fail to prevent colic, read and re-read all my instructions on feeding and compare them carefully with what you are doing. CONTACT me if there are no satisfactory results. I can be contacted via my publishers whose address is given on page ii.

The prevention of colic; screaming two hours after food, with delay in bringing up wind, and crying into the night (with under-feeding the baby cries out of the night) both are dealt with in the instructions on feeding.

Do not ignore colic, it has far reaching effects. Even up to three years of age, and is one of the major causes of Battered Babies due to loss of sleep, a persistently crying baby and a physically worn out mother! No matter what she does her baby still cries. Colic can destroy an otherwise happy family life.

I do not blame the parents for battering a baby but I do blame the people who fail to advise how to overcome this particular condition.

§

30

DISCOMFORT

1. An open safety pin sticking into the babe.
2. Tapes or nappies etc. fastened too tightly.
3. Some nightdresses have a girdle. Should this be tied in a knot the baby may be lying on it.
4. The babe may require change of position. See Two Hourly Routine (No 46). Also a change of nappy.
5. All the other reasons for crying.

This chapter excludes all other crying causes numbers 1-10 except number 8.

Safety pins without the slip safety catch carry a certain amount of risk. Regardless whether "Safe" or open pins are used it is important that the nappy is pinned with the pin going ACROSS the body and NOT up and down. This ensures that an open pin does not push into the baby's abdomen when the baby pulls up his legs, especially when he is crying.

When ties, especially around nightdresses and adjustable "Tie Plastic Pants", are fastened BEFORE a feed they may cause discomfort as the abdomen is swollen after a feed, causing tightness.

Always lie the baby on his right side after a feed to prevent discomfort. The stomach is on his left side and after a feed it is swollen. Lying on his left side can cause uncomfortable pressure. Lie the baby on the left side after giving water. This prevents uneven development of the left and right side of the head and body.

To avoid knots, as on nightdresses, it is best to avoid belts. They are not really necessary.

Requiring a change of position is capable of causing distress. Adults automatically change position. A young baby is incapable of doing so. The two hourly routine during the day will prevent this and the crying for a soiled or wet nappy.

The baby may also be cold, requiring more covering or the covering tucked more firmly around his neck. This is so important.

§

31

HUNGER

1. A correctly fed babe commences to become restless for food approximately three to five minutes BEFORE a feed is due.
2. Crying earlier than that, (providing the babe is not thirsty) indicates at that particular feed more food is required.
3. This only happens at an odd feed and not necessary every feed.
4. The cry is lusty, accompanied by vigorous kicking.
5. If breast fed it is a sign the milk is failing at that particular feed.
6. Step up the intake of stout.
7. For a very young breast fed baby give some whey. If older, some diluted cow's milk until the breast milk is restored.
8. For artificial feeding add half an ounce (1.5 cls) of extra food.
9. Refer to Underfeeding (No 27) and other notes (Nos 38-39).

I have placed this reason for crying nearly at the end of the list to get things into perspective. The majority of babies are over-fed: Hunger is one of the last reasons for crying.

Initially presume thirst.

This is when Clock Feeding (No 46) really comes into its own!

Should the baby be crying 15 minutes before a feed it is a sign of hunger.

In the case of a breast fed baby the problem is easily rectified. The mother has been probably doing chores or perhaps shopping. A rest and a glass of stout on her return will solve the problem of the 2.00 pm feed.

An artificially fed babe usually has the five feeds a day adjustment after being weighed. Occasionally the babe may require an extra half ounce (1.5 cls) at a particular feed. The next day add that extra half ounce to that feed.

The cry is always lusty accompanied by vigorous kicking and the throwing about of arms. Other times the baby is quiet. The weight gain is normal. So different from the under-fed baby who has a weak continuous cry, scant and rather green stools and, of course, poor weight gain. The baby is under weight.

REMEMBER the baby should ONLY BE TWICE the birth weight at the age of six months.

§

32

LONELINESS

1. A young baby is not lonely.
2. A young baby sleeps 22 hours out of twenty four hours.
3. As the weeks go by the baby will lie awake for longer periods but is capable of amusing himself, especially outside watching the trees etc.
4. As the "Awake" time lengthens the baby does like company when in the house.

This is a problem of the older baby, the toddler, the juvenile and the teenager.

A very young babe requires 22 hours sleep per day. This allows for five feeds and time for a nappy change. The baby is nursed when fed, and of course spoken to. At this early stage the baby becomes familiar with sounds and intonations of the human voice. During the early weeks this is sufficient.

At the age of about three months, the age may vary a little, the baby requires human company and is capable of becoming restless especially when voices or footsteps are heard.

A familiar slogan is "Cuddle your baby" but it should be "Talk to your baby!" Speech is far more important! When cuddling is excessive the mother has the tendency to spoil the child and to become over protective and possessive.

When the child becomes too old for cuddling, with conversation lacking, direct contact is broken, resulting in the "Teenagers Warcry" – "I can't talk to my parents they do not understand."

Parents, on the other hand who have had the older baby around, can chatter to their baby while working. Soon their babe will respond with "Cooing" and other sounds according to age and ability. The contact is speech which comes naturally from the earliest age.

Toddlers, as we all know, asked repeated questions until one could scream. Do not scream, just say "yes" or "no", "don't know!!" So long as they have a response they are usually content. To them an unsatisfactory answer will always bring forth a comment or another question. They proceed accordingly.

The cuddling stage has passed at approximately seven years. Do not worry. Parents who have had the contact of speech for these seven years have nothing to fear. The child keeps his self respect in front of others, yet retains confidence in the parents during his childhood trials and tribulations.

Cuddle your child by all means, should he want you to do so, but remember, speech must last during the child's life until the end of your own. Then they can say "My parents were the best in the world."

33

COLOSTRUM

1. This is the food Nature intended for the baby for the first three days after birth.
2. Colostrum only needs absorbing by the digestive system.
3. It works in conjunction with the meconeum (the black stool) – acts as a mild aperient.
4. Colostrum is present in the quantity that Nature intended.
5. It educates the body to digest and absorb food.

Colostrum is the perfect food after a baby is born. It contains approximately twice as much protein as breast milk. Although in small quantities it is much more sustaining than breast milk. As it is so nutritious it gradually educates the baby to coping with life. After all a baby, until born, has never had to digest food.

Once food is taken the whole digestive system reacts, the bowel containing the soft lubricating meconeum,(the black stool), is gradually expelled, followed by the products of the small amounts of colostrum. How gently Nature provides for her precious baby.

Some babies do not have the good fortune to be breast fed. WHEY is the best substitute for 24 hours after birth – but this is entirely up to the midwife. The left over curd may be used as cream cheese for the adults, flavoured to taste with chopped chives, beetroot, onion, apricot and so on.

34

EXPRESSION OF BREASTS

1. Learn how to express your breasts.
2. Ask the Staff Midwife in hospital, District Midwife or Health Visitor how to do it, and if necessary, to show you how.
3. The expression of breasts is a knack! Have patience and DON'T wait until it is necessary before you develop the art, because an art it is!
4. Providing you intend breast feeding your baby, order, in early pregnancy, a breast pump from your chemist.
5. As soon as the milk comes into the breasts, be it day or night, use the breast pump and so preventing engorged breasts.
6. Some hospitals have automatic breast pumps. At home you have not.

It is very important that this art is acquired before one leaves hospital. After a home confinement the Domicilliary Midwife will have time and patience to help you during the difficult period. Should you still not have acquired the knack, ask your Health Visitor. Do appreciate the fact she has more time than anyone in the hospital to help you.

After confinement it can be days or weeks before they become engorged. Providing you have a breast pump or you can manually express your breasts, it is possible to prevent the discomfort of engorged breasts, or even worse, a breast abscess.

These conditions are more than painful, they are agonising! The result is a screaming hungry baby and a mother in tears with pain and frustration. Many babies are put onto the bottle for just this reason, in spite of the mother's wish to breast feed. What a loss to the baby and, of course the mother who loses her contact.

The main advice I give is avoid engorgement by using the breast pump, WHEN NECESSARY, BEFORE A FEED NEVER AFTER and between feeds if necessary until the routine of feeding has become established.

Again I say one breast one feed can prevent engorgement and perhaps later a breast abscess.

ALWAYS USE A GOOD SUPPORTING BRA.

ENGORGED BREASTS

1. Read the chapter on Immediately After the Baby is Born (Nos 18-21).
2. Read the chapter on Social Life While Breast Feeding (No 37).
3. One breast, one feed empties the breast. Therefore preventing engorgement. (The demand equals the supply plus half a feed in reserve).
4. A mother with her first babe may have difficulty in fixing her babe on to one of her breasts. This depends whether she is left or right handed.
5. ALWAYS start off on that "Difficult" breast until the babe fixes properly.
6. The use of a firm supporting bra is very comforting and can either prevent engorgement or help should it occur.
7. Cracked nipples.
8. From now on breast feeding should continue uninterrupted.
9. Take your stout regularly unless there is any medical reason why you should not.

This is a very painful condition and to be avoided at all costs. Again – easy when you know how! This happens usually with first babies.

Once the breasts are emptied the supply equals the demand. A breast pump is a great help but it is useless using it after the baby is fed because it will not empty the breasts even though you are unable to express any more milk. ONLY the baby can empty the breast. Use the pump BEFORE a feed.

Use the *sterile* glass piece of the breast pump before you commence feeding. use a *sterile funnel* and pour the expressed milk into a bottle in case you need it. THIS IS AN EXCELLENT TIME TO COMMENCE ONE BREAST, ONE FEED, and no further trouble.

One breast one feed, is also more than useful, for instance, in the Summer, when travelling in a car. There is nothing worse than this mode of travel for dehydrating a mother, consequently the milk supply diminishes. The half feed in reserve comes to the rescue and tides you over the emergency. Plenty of water at the end of your journey soon brings you back to normal.

ALWAYS use a deep supportive bra – even during the night.

§

36

CRACKED NIPPLES

CAUSES:

1. Inadequate care of nipples during pregnancy.
2. Allowing the child to fall asleep at the breast.
3. Too frequent feeding, (poor milk supply).
4. Prolonged sucking at an empty breast, (poor milk supply).
5. Not drinking stout.

Cracked nipples, like any other complaint, can vary in severity. They can even bleed as the baby is sucking.

The fist thing to do is MANUALLY express the breasts. This is important as the use of a breast exhaust opens up the cracks.

This manual expression is time-consuming until you become super-efficient. Give the expressed milk to the baby using a feeding bottle with a small-holed teat.

KNEAD some ointment into the nipples. This may prove painful at the beginning. If the ointment is just rubbed on the chances are the nipples could break down again once the babe is put to the breast.

Once the nipples are sufficiently healed when kneaded on the application of the ointment refer to the article Preparation of the Nipples (No 13).

When you have reached this stage the babe may be put to the breast AFTER you have expressed them. The baby will empty the breasts. This will help to restore the milk supply. If there are no ill effects you may return to the normal routine.

SOCIAL LIFE WHILE BREAST FEEDING

1. It is always useful to have in reserve two full feeding bottles of breast milk.
2. Keep sterilised a small plastic funnel.
3. BEFORE each feed draw off from each breast some milk using the sterile base of the breast pump.
4. Pour into a sterile feeding bottle using the sterile funnel.
5. Keep the bottles in the cold part of the fridge.
6. When the required bottles are full, dispose of the first one.
7. There is always extra milk should the occasion arise.
8. It saves bothering with artificial feeding.
9. It is useful to feed one breast, one feed.
10. It is important, when at home for feeds, the baby is allowed to empty the breasts to avoid a breast abscess. Express the breast beforehand if necessary.

This chapter, I hope, will be of assistance to those mothers whose lives, whatever they may be, make it obligatory for them to attend public functions. Many of you in this position either fail to breast feed or do so for a very short period. This situation, to say the least, can be distressing, especially when the mothers are keen.

The notes on this subject give instructions as to how this can be achieved. The main thing is to feed one breast one feed, thus ensuring always a half feed in reserve. Some say this method makes one feel lopsided. At the beginning it may do so, but one gets used to it.

It is important to USE A SMALL-HOLED TEAT. Breast milk is thin. Breast milk given through a medium-holed teat will give the baby colic.

Refer to Results of Wrong Feeding. (Nos 49-58).

ARTIFICIAL FEEDING

38

HOW TO CALCULATE THE AMOUNT OF MILK REQUIRED

1. A baby requires $2^{1}/_{2}$ oz (7.0 cls) of food in the 24 hours to EACH POUND (0.45 kg) of its body weight without clothes. Irrespective of three or four hourly feeds.
2. EXAMPLE 1.
a. A baby weighs 6 lb (2.7 kg) at birth.
b. $2^{1}/_{2}$ oz (7.0 cls) x 6 lb (2.7kg) = 15 oz (43 cls)
c. 4 hourly feeds = 5 feeds a day = 15 oz (43 cls) divided by 5 oz = 3 oz (9.0 cls) each feed – NO NIGHT FEEDING.
d. 3-hourly feeds = 6 feeds a day = 15 oz (43 cls)divided by 6 =$2^{1}/_{2}$ oz (7.0 cls) each feed. NO NIGHT FEEDING.
3. EXAMPLE 2.
a. A baby weighs 10 lb (4.6 kg) at birth.
b. $2^{1}/_{2}$ oz (7.0cls) x 10lb (4.6 kg) = 25 oz (71 cls) in the 24 hours.
c. 4-hourly feeds = 5 feeds a day = 25 oz (71 cls) divided by 5 = 5 oz (14 cls) each feed. NO NIGHT FEEDING.
d. 3-hourly feeds = 6 feeds a day = 5 feeds of 4 oz (12 cls) + one feed of 5 oz (14 cls). Preferably given as the last feed. NO NIGHT FEEDING.

FEEDING
4. Milk required for the odd $^{1}/_{4}$, $^{1}/_{2}$, $^{3}/_{4}$ lb body weight
    lb oz
    6. 0 (2.72 kg) requires 15 oz (43 cls) in 24 hours
    6. 4 (2.84 kg) requires $15^{1}/_{4}$oz (44 cls) in 24 hours
    6. 8 (2.95 kg) requires $16^{1}/_{2}$ oz (47 cls) in 24 hours
    6. 12 (3.12 kg) requires 17 oz (48 cls) in 24 hours
    7. 0 (3.28 kg) requires $17^{1}/_{4}$ oz (50 cls) in 24 hours
    7. 4 (3.29 kg) requires 18 oz (51 cls) in 24 hours
    7. 8 (3.40 kg) requires 19 oz (54 cls) in 24 hours

lb oz

7. 12 (3.6 kg)	requires 19½ oz (55 cls) in 24 hours
8. 0 (3.63 kg)	requires 20 oz (57 cls) in 24 hours
8. 4 (3.9 kg)	requires 20½ oz (58 cls) in 24 hours
8. 8 (3.93 kg)	requires 21½ oz (61 cls) in 24 hours
8. 12 (4.0 kg)	requires 22 oz (63 cls) in 24 hours
9. 0 (4.1 kg)	requires 22½ oz (64 cls) in 24 hours
9. 4 (4.2 kg)	requires 23 oz (65 cls) in 24 hours
9. 8 (4.3 kg)	requires 24 oz (68 cls) in 24 hours
9. 12 (4.4 kg)	requires 24½ oz (70 cls) in 24 hours
10. 0 (4.5 kg)	requires 25 oz (71 cls) in 24 hours
10. 4 (4.7 kg)	requires 25½ oz (72 cls) in 24 hours
10. 8 (4.8 kg)	requires 26½ oz (76 cls) in 24 hours
10. 12 (4.9 kg)	requires 27 oz (77 cls) in 24 hours
11. 0 (5.0 kg)	requires 27½ oz (78 cls) in 24 hours

I have compiled a detailed chart of a baby's weight gain and the gradual increase in the amount of food required according to the 4 oz (113gms), 8 oz (228gms) and 12 oz (340gms) weight which you will observe is the same increase regardless of the weight of the child.

When the babe is born refer to the chart (birth weight) and proceed from there. I have taken the weight up to 11.0 lb (5.0 kg). These increases MUST BE ADHERED TO until the babe at THE AGE OF SIX MONTHS has doubled his birth weight WITHOUT SOLIDS.

Some older babies on their own accord put themselves onto four feeds a day. This is no problem provided the overall quantity of milk taken is the correct amount according to the weight of the baby.

I again draw your attention to the fact that ABOVE normal weight gain means LACK OF WATER and the baby is trying to quench his thirst on milk. This in turn causes problems; strong urine, sore buttocks and so on.

WEIGHT GAIN DURING THE FIRST YEAR OF LIFE

BIRTH WEIGHT		6 MONTHS		12 MONTHS	
lb	kg	lb	kg	lb	kg
6	(2.75)	12	(5.5)	18	(8.2)
6 1/2	(2.9)	13	(5.9)	19 1/2	(8.9)
7	(3.2)	14	(6.4)	21	(9.5)
8	(3.6)	16	(7.3)	24	(10.9)
9	(4.1)	18	(8.2)	27	(12.4)
9 1/2	(4.4)	19	(8.7)	28 1/2	(13.0)
10	(4.5)	20	(9.1)	30	(13.6)
10 1/2	(4.9)	21	(9.7)	31 1/2	(14.3)

WEEKLY GAINS

1	6 lb	–	3 3/4 oz	(106 gms)
2	6 1/2 lb	–	4 oz	(113 gms)
3	7 lb	–	4 1/2 oz	(127 gms)
4	8 lb	–	5 oz -	(142 gms)
5	9 1/2 lb	–	6 oz	(170 gms)
6	10 lb	–	6 ozs +	(175 gms)
7	10 1/2 lb	–	6 1/2 oz	(184 gms)

I hope that the table of weight gains explains why some babies are so much larger than others and gain more than others per week. When the age and weight does not coincide with the birth weight it means over-feeding *or* under-feeding. USUALLY over-feeding. On average a 6lb baby increases in weight by 6 lb in 6 months. To calculate the average *weekly gain* weight, the *birth* weight in ounces (there are 16 oz in 1 lb) is divided by 26 (26 weeks in six months, 52 in one year).

As a result of all this do not be impressed with a "Big Baby". This idea has come from days gone by when babies became infected with tuberculosis for which there was no cure. These babies "faded away"; this meant that so long as a baby put on lots of weight it was "healthy", in other words he did not suffer from tuberculosis, although it was not said in so many words. Should the babe contract tuberculosis or some other debilitating illness he had "something to lose".

Children these days do not usually contract tuberculosis, thanks to TT milk which is also pasteurised. Should they do so there are drugs to cure it.

An over heavy baby is DANGEROUS! Repeated bronchitis and danger of pneumonia. This, in later life, means a chronic bronchitic and often a sufferer from emphysema, a terrible chest condition – and THIS IS WHERE IT STARTS – AN OVERWEIGHT BABY! It is better to have your baby slightly underweight. IT IS SAFER.

§

40

STOOLS OF A YOUNG BABY

1. NORMAL: Yellow, consistency of freshly mixed mustard.
2. TOO MUCH SUGAR: like separated scrambled egg, and frothy with a very faint tinge of green perhaps.
3. CONSTIPATED:
    (a) Pale yellow and peels off napkin.
    (b) Streaked with red and hard.
4. GREEN: if scanty, under-fed or baby has cold etc.
5. GREEN DIARRHOEA:
    (a) Infection due to lack of cleanliness.
    (b) If violent diarrhoea, gastro-enteritis. Refer to chapter on Gastro-enteritis (No 55).
6. VERY BULKY AND PALE:Coelic Disease (fat intolerance), a medical condition requiring medical treatment.

The notes give a general guide to the types of different stools and what they signify. Most of them are dealt with in feeding and I have given a clue as to where the information can be found.

The very bulky pale stools are mentioned to raise your suspicions suggesting Coelic Disease. If in doubt, ask your Health Visitor. The baby is an unhappy baby. I do not expect you to be worrying about every soiled nappy you change, I am only trying to help you to be observant and leave the worrying to your Health Visitor.

The gastro-enteritis has been dealt with in another chapter. Any suspicions you may have, save the soiled nappies from that time on. Replace the previous soiled nappy with the fresh one. This means when your Health Visitor calls there is a soiled nappy on hand for inspection.

§

41

THE RECONSTITUTION OF DRIED MILK

1. These instructions for the reconstitution of dried milk DEMAND CLOCK FEEDING.
2. Read EACH article in this book on feeding, both breast and artificial and especially the one on Clock Feeding (No 46).
3. Measure the milk according to the instructions on the packet. For example 4 x measures of powder to 4 oz (12 cls) of water.
4. ADD another 2 oz (6.0 cls) of water making 4 x measures of powder and 6 oz (17 cls) of water.
5. Compare the density of this mixture with cow's milk. Should the baby's milk have the "plop, plop" of emulsion paint, add 1 oz (28 ml) of extra water.
6. Shake again. Add extra water if necessary.
7. From this quantity measure the amount of feed required.
8. The sucking time using a small-holed teat MUST be 20 minutes REGARDLESS OF THE AMOUNT of food and the size of the baby.
9. The feed should satisfy the babe for four hours.
10. If the sucking time is less than 20 minutes, reduce the water per feed by 1/2 oz (1.5 cls) until 20 minutes sucking time is achieved.
11. ON NO ACCOUNT ADD EXTRA POWDER TO THIS MIXTURE.
12. When – and only when, the satisfactory measurements are obtained, CONTINUE to mix the food in batches of 4 x scoops of milk powder to your own amount of water.
13. Increase the babe's feed as required but NOT the QUALITY.
14. THE SAME PERSON MUST ALWAYS MEASURE THE DRIED MILK.

Those "Clinging" milk powders are very difficult to measure accurately. Depending how hard an individual "Digs" into the packet of milk depends the quantity of powder squashed into the scoop. I have known mothers who used a well known brand of milk manage to cram TWO measures of food into one scoop! but only reconstitute it with the recommended quantity of water. Needless to say, the babes had violent colic due to the very thick food. This mixture requires a LARGE-holed teat and the babes were sleepy feeders. Instead of one measure of food to 1 oz of water (3.0 cls), one measure of food to two ounces (6.0 cls) of water was called for. Once that was sorted out – no more colic!

Of course, not everyone manages to pack the powder so tightly, but very few people measure the powder accurately. Fewer still know how to adjust their incorrect measurements to the normal consistency by adding extra water and then comparing it with cow's milk.

Half fill a feeding bottle with cow's milk and another feeding bottle, half full of YOUR mixture. Shake both simultaneously. The cow's milk leaves the sides of the bottle. The dried milk mixture, if too thick, will cling to the side. There is also the "Plop, plop" feel and sound. There is no mistaking this when you experience it. How much like "Emulsion paint" depends on the thickness of the food.

It is a good idea, after you have added the extra 2 oz (6.0 cls) of water to the ordinary mixture to add extra water by the $1/2$oz (1.5 cls) at a time. This method prevents you over-diluting the food. Should this happen you MUST begin again and of course the food is wasted. From this special mixture measure the baby's feed. If correct, feed is 20 minutes sucking time, using a SMALL-holed teat, and the babe should be satisfied for four hours. Should the babe becomes restless, give a drink of plain boiled water. Make certain you "Wind" the baby thoroughly.

Continue to make up the mixture in this quantity NEVER LESS. Do not discard the extra, use it for the next feed. NEVER ADD EXTRA POWDER TO THE MIXTURE. ONLY REDUCE WATER.

Should the babe become restless before the four hours and you have already given a drink of water, increase the feed by $1/2$oz (1.5 cls). If the babe refuses the extra it is a sign the food is too weak. Cut down the water from your basic mixture by $1/2$oz until the babe is settled. Also refer to the weight chart.

Do not be alarmed if your friend uses more or less water to 4 x scoops. She may have a lighter or heavier hand when it comes to measuring the dried milk.

No matter how small or large the baby, the same rule applies. NEVER make a richer food, except when following these instructions. IT IS FATAL!

NEVER be slip-shod measuring dried milk. If in doubt, for example losing count, begin again – and I mean that! In a day or two every mum will become a first-class "measurer".

ONLY ONE PERSON TO MEASURE THE DRIED MILK.

The only way the baby can say "Thank you" for your trouble is by not having to cry because of colic. Surely that is enough!

§

42

TO COUNTER CHECK THE CORRECT MEASURE OF DRIED MILK.

1. Check your method with my instructions in every detail, no matter what brand of milk you use.
2. Should the baby cry two hours after food (colic), the food is too thick, in spite of your care and what you may think!
3. It is one thing to demonstrate how to measure dried milk and another thing to write it down for you to understand.
4. A first class guide is to have a feeding bottle containing cow's milk in it and another feeding bottle with your particular brand of milk in it.
5. Lift the two bottles to just above eye level and SHAKE.
6. The cow's milk immediately drains from the side of the bottle.
7. The dried milk should do the same, and no "Plop, plop" when shaken as if the dried milk was emulsion paint.

This is more or less a repeat of the measuring of dried milk. No one can be too careful when preparing this milk. You just have to read the article on Results of Wrong Feeding, (Nos 49-58), to fully appreciate the importance of correct measuring. Read also The Cries of a Baby, Nos 22-32), should you be in any doubt as to the cause of the crying. The sucking time and the crying time are the two most important factors to ascertain whether you are measuring the food correctly and adding sufficient water to the measured powder.

I must stress – during all your counter-checking DO NOT RULE OUT THIRST, especially if the weather or the environment is warm. After you have ruled out thirst, the babe may require just 1/2oz (1.5 cls) more food. Clock Feeding (No 46) will explain this to you.

A final check, DO NOT FORGET to compare the cow's milk and the dried milk by shaking each bottle. Once you have become efficient measuring single feeds correctly, the food may be mixed all in one for 24 hours. STERILE diabetic scales may be used to weigh the powder rather than run the risk of losing count of the number of scoops if distracted. These scales are accurate for measuring small quantities.

§

43

ADAPTION OF COW'S MILK

1. 10 oz (28.5 cls)) of SKIMMED cow's milk.
2. 1 oz (28 gms) sugar.
3. 1 oz (3.0 cls) single cream.
4. Water UP TO 1 pint, (57 cls).

METHOD

1. COMMENCE with the 28.5 cls of skimmed cow's milk.
2. Add the sugar, and cream to the milk.
3. Add water UP TO 1 PINT.
4. DO NOT COMMENCE WITH 10 oz (28.5 cls) OF WATER.
5. This makes 1 pint (57.0 cls) of mixture.
6. Mix total quantity required to the nearest 10 oz (28.5 cls).
7. Pour the mixture into five bottles – five feeds.
8. Place a plate or terry towelling at the bottom of the pan or pressure cooker to prevent breakage.
9. Place the bottles in the pan and cold water up to the level of the milk.
10. Bring to boil and boil for 15 minutes.

11. Should the bottles be narrow necked, plug with cotton wool and leave in.
12. Wide necked bottles, screw on caps with 1/2 turn.
13. Tighten screws afterwards.
14. Reduce heat gradually but as quickly as possible. Stand in cold running water before placing into the fridge.

This is a very useful method in rural areas when, owing to storm or lack of transport, the usual milk supply fails to get through.

Adding only water to cow's milk is not suitable for infants, except when used for an odd feed.

There is too much protein for an infant in undiluted cow's milk. When diluted the cream and sugar are reduced to below the required amount, therefore extra sugar and cream must be added.

It is necessary to keep the infant on this mixture until the age of 4 1/2 months. Then gradually increase the mixture to full cow's milk.

§

44

HOW TO KEEP MILK FRESH

METHOD 1

1. Make a half bucketful of a saturated solution of washing soda.
2. Put three handfuls of washing soda into the bucket.
3. Add APPROXIMATELY 1 pint (57.0 cls) of boiling water and stir.
4. Leave for 24 hours. Add another handful of soda and another pint or less of boiling water and stir.
5. Leave for another 24 hours. There should be some crystals remaining in the bottom of the bucket. (Saturated solution.)
6. Do not repeat if quantity is sufficient.
7. Add water as the water evaporates.
8. Always leave some crystals in the bucket.
9. Place the covered milk container in the bucket, UP to the level of the milk.

10. Cover the bucket to keep the dust out.
11. Renew the solution periodically.

METHOD 2

1. Make a strong solution of Baking Soda (Bicarbonate of Soda) dissolved in boiling water.
2. Add one or two teaspoonfuls of solution to the milk.
3. Stir well and taste.
4. Wash spoon after each tasting.
5. Add another one or two teaspoonfuls of the solution, stir and taste.
6. Repeat until one is JUST CONSCIOUS of the flavour of the soda bicarb. Then stop. (Note the quantity used for one pint – 57.0 cls – of milk.)
7. Repeated tasting renders the palate sensitive to the flavour of soda bicarb.
8. Milk thus treated does not flavour tea, coffee or food.
9. This mixture can be used for infants, WITH SAFETY.

These methods of preserving the freshness of milk are useful in homes, caravans and areas where there is no refrigeration. The two methods combined is even more effective than using just one or other method alone, and the combined method is resistant against the hottest weather.

Method 1 can be used to keep other food fresh, providing a water-tight container is used.

EVAPORATED MILK

1. As a rule evaporated milk is measured one part of milk to two parts of water. 5 oz (14.0 cls) of milk to 10 oz (28.0 cls) of water.
2. Some babies are unable to tolerate this mixture.
3. Usually I advise from the start one part milk to three parts water; 5 oz (14.0 cls) of milk to 15 oz (3/4 pint , (43.0 cls)) of water.
4. Be guided by weight gain, crying after food and To Counter Check the Correct Measuring of Dried Milk. (No 42), and others.

This method is quite good because the measuring is so simple. The main thing to remember is to ADD water to MILK and NOT vice-versa and that is AFTER you have added the sugar. Like the adaption of cow's milk, the melted sugar measures part of 1 oz (3.0 cls).

One of the snags of this method is the carrying home of a number of tins of milk, making it an extra heavy shopping basket.

MANNER OF FEEDING

46

CLOCK FEEDING

1. This means feeding at the *same hour* each day.
2. Excellent. This method tells one why a baby is crying.
3. Should a baby sleep or lie quietly for five hours, (except during the night), too much food has been given at the last feed.
4. Should the babe become restless after 3 1/2 hours (4 hourly feeds) presume thirst. After that it means the babe requires more food at that particular feed. 4 oz (11.0 cls) food lasts for four hours, therefore 3 oz (9.0 cls)of food lasts for three hours in the early stages.
5. In breast fed babes 20 minutes sucking time lasts four hours. Be guided by the clock.
6. When commencing this routine, give as much food as the baby will take, then calculate the time the baby remains quiet.
7. If the baby wakes at 7.00 am instead of 6.00 am, give 3 oz (9.0 cls) of boiled water, followed immediately by a three hour feed. This means the baby will awake at 10.00 am for the next feed, as planned.
8. A baby can be organised into any routine.
9. A planned routine is ESSENTIAL for the self-employed or working managers. For instance, Newsagents. I mention newsagents as the perfect example of what I wish to illustrate. The feed is given at 9.00 pm then 4.30 am when they rise to cope with the daily papers etc. The next feed is 10.00 am after the busy morning period followed by a feed at 2.00 pm and 6.00 pm.

It is the cry of the breast feeding mothers that they do not know how much the baby is taking. The clock will tell you.

There is one problem which I must mention and that is the babe who wakens at, for instance, 9.00 pm instead of 9.30 pm ready for 10.00 pm feed. Give less water at 6.00 pm which the baby takes a little extra food to last the extra 1/2 hour. Keep the baby waiting for half an hour by nursing and talking to him. This wait makes him very hungry and he is prepared to take a large feed. Naturally working this way will take longer than the other way, but do not be discouraged. Have patience and you will achieve the desired results. Watch the clock and be guided by it.

When a mother is discharged from hospital on the Saturday or a Bank Holiday I have visited on the Tuesday morning and been greeted by a mother in tears, worn out with lack of sleep and a crying baby, usually fed on demand. Once a mother reaches this stage it takes two or three weeks to get the mother and baby settled.

This is why I say it is so essential to start the routine you wish to continue with immediately after birth. It is so easy then. After all, why run the risk of all this frustration when you need not!!

The waking (not crying) and sleeping time is governed by the amount of food taken; five hours sleep means too much food; crying three and a half hours after food of half an hour before means thirst or requiring 1/2 oz (1.5 cls)more food.

I shall deal with Failure of Breast Milk and Crying Between Feeds elsewhere.

Clock feeding, which is feeding the baby at the SAME hour EACH DAY, DOES NOT MEAN the babe cries incessantly until the feeding time comes round. Should this be the case there is something radically wrong with management somewhere along the line.

I shall work on the usual four hourly routine; 6.00 am, 10.00 am, 2.00 pm, 6.00 pm and 10.00 pm. What I am going to say applies also to the three hourly routine but I shall deal more fully with that later in the book.

Should the babe waken at, say, 11.00 am instead of 10.00 am for his bath it is quite easy to give 3 oz (9.0 cls) of water and follow immediately by an ounce less food so that he is awake at 2.00 pm. If the child wakens later than 6.00 am the next morning give a drink of water and a small feed the child is awake at 10.00 am. Within approximately two feeds the babe will have arrived at the set feed time. In the case of breast feeding, give the water and approximately five minutes less feeding time. More than likely the baby will automatically take less. Feed the baby *before* the bath – he is not going to swim a marathon!

The average sucking time is 20 minutes, but there are very few exceptions to this rule. When I was a Pupil Midwife, an 11lb (5.0 kg) baby was born and breast fed. From 9.00 pm until 5.30 am that poor baby screamed all night because she was overfed. Unbeknown to the Hierarchy I test-weighed the baby. In case I was caught tampering with the feeds I had to prove myself. In 10 minutes sucking time that babe was getting 12oz (34.0 cls) of food. No wonder the babe screamed! I cut down the breast feed to five minutes. No more trouble. This explains why it is so essential to check sucking time with the contented time.

§

47

HOW TO CUT OUT NIGHT FEEDING FROM BIRTH

1. THE FOLLOWING INSTRUCTIONS MUST BE CARRIED OUT EXACTLY (otherwise it does not work.)
2. At 6.00 pm feed give approximately 3 oz (86 ml) or more of boiled water (no sugar) in a bottle with a small-holed teat.
3. Follow IMMEDIATELY with a small feed, (approximately 1 oz less or a shorter feed if breast feeding).
4. The feed should be small enough to make sure the baby is awake at 9.30 pm. This is adjusted by the amount of water given at 6.00 pm.
5. Nurse and talk to the baby until 10.00 pm.
6. The babe having to wait for a feed is wide awake and hungry.
7. Because he is wide awake and hungry he will take an extra large feed. Give him as much as he will take.
8. This extra feed carries the baby past 2.00 am.
9. Take to bed with you a hot water bottle wrapped in a shawl, and keep it in your bed.
10. Have the cot next to, and touching, your bed – VERY IMPORTANT.
11. When the baby becomes restless, approximately 3.00 - 3.30 am, DO NOT TALK, DO NOT PUT THE LIGHT ON.
12. Take the warm shawl, lift up the corner of the covers, slip it under the covers.
13. RESULT the baby will calm down and sleep until 6.00 am.

14. I say three nights will settle the babe. It is usually two.
15. Continue with the hot water bottle and shawl until you have had four consecutive undisturbed nights sleep.
16. After four undisturbed nights sleep the babe can go into his own room, if he has one.
17. On cold nights an extra cover put onto the cot after the 10.00 pm feed will ensure that the baby remains warm and asleep throughout the night.
18. Should the baby waken at 5.30 am the baby is short of approximately 1/2 oz (1.5 cls) of food at 10.00 pm. Give *more* water and *less* food at 6.00 pm.

Night feeding means to the mother the loss of sleep to the tune of FOURTEEN hours a week. Especially when the baby is bottle fed. You may be surprised at this but let me explain. You become aware of the baby beginning to wriggle, you wonder whether he will waken up. Then you have to heat a feed, then feed and wind the babe, then change the nappy, and lie wondering whether he will settle afterwards. AND how long it takes YOU to settle. By the time this ritual is gone through, time yourself and you will find it is very near two hours a night. Losing this sleep every night for two, three, four weeks or longer it is physically impossible for the mother to do justice to the baby, herself or other members of the household.

Apart from this – NIGHT FEEDING IS NOT NECESSARY, EVEN WITH A SMALL BABY OR WHEN THREE HOURLY FEEDS ARE GIVEN. Each baby's tummy is large enough to sustain its body through the night. We do not feed during the night just because we are not the size of elephants!

The drink of water at 6.00 pm not only prevents crying from thirst, it also makes sure the baby is satisfied with a small 6.00 pm feed. Without the drink of water the babe will not accept a small feed. Because of not having a small feed the baby is not awake at 9.30 pm. Not being awake at 9.30 pm he will not take that extra large feed at 10.00 pm and no amount of warm shawls may keep that baby asleep throughout the night. The warm shawl may keep the baby asleep for another hour but he will be awake at approximately 4.00 am. Mark my words! So do not omit that drink of water at 6.00 pm.

The other point I would like to emphasize is having the cot next to your bed. If not the baby can hear and feel you moving because the carpet and floorboards conduct the vibration of your steps and vibrate the baby's cot. In other words you are pipped at the post! Once the babe is awake you are compelled to feed him. As a midwife in hospital walking towards the nursery, every baby was yelling – I stopped dead and in about three seconds there was silence! One could hear a pin drop. Within another three seconds or less the full chorus resumed; illustrating how sensitive a baby is to sound and vibration.

§

48

DEMAND FEEDING

1. Not good
2. The baby suffers too much while getting into a routine.
3. It is difficult to arrive at the reason for a baby crying (there are 11 reasons.)
4. The routine the babe gets into may not be suitable, for example, newsagents with unusual hours.
5. You are unable to plan your life.
6. Tendency for the baby to become a slow feeder.
7. A little and often.
8. Tendency to sore nipples (Refer to Cracked Nipples, No 36.)

This is a good method if mothers were sheep with nothing to do but feed one's self and feed the lamb, but they are not sheep and, therefore unable to feed a baby while at the same time carrying out daily commitments satisfactorily.

A baby comes into the world not knowing anything about it. He will be prepared, with help, to be moulded into any routine. Demand feeding is like going into an entirely new job without help. As though a musician is directed to an architect's office and just told to get on with it. Like the baby, the musician will suffer by mistakes until he has learnt how to cope. Anyone will agree this method is anything but satisfactory. It is frustrating and tiring.

In under developed countries the babies do not suffer because there are more experienced members of the family to look after them and consequently the family routine is not disrupted.

In modern society a disrupted family routine results in an over-tired mother who will eventually become a Martyr-to-the-Cause. The over-tired mother and a restless baby are two difficult people to live with and all to no purpose.

One loses one's friends. When friends are being entertained and about to sit down to a meal, the baby cries. No one wants to eat while the hostess is absent. Result, a spoilt meal and a frustrated hostess.

There is another reason possibly causing lack of relaxation, puerperal depression and, possibly, a battered baby.

Refer to Results of Wrong Feeding (Nos 49-58).

Having the wee one awake at 9.30pm means the evening meal has already been eaten – and in peace. The visitors, parents and especially the father – who is usually out at work has the opportunity to nurse and amuse the babe until the 10pm feed.

RESULTS OF WRONG FEEDING

1. Slow feeding
2. Babe not taking the full amount.
3. Colic (crying two hours after food).
4. Cries mistaken for hunger.
5. Difficult winding.
6. Solids given too early.
7. Strong Urine
8. Sore buttocks.
9. Difficulty in forming a feeding routine.
10. Persistent large weight gain.
11. Overweight baby.
12. Gripe water to the fore.
13. Chesty cold and perhaps, pneumonia.
14. Extra sugar added to the feed to relieve constipation, resulting in too much sugar.
15. Poor sleep – hyper-activity.

Very seldom is an artificially fed baby under-fed at the beginning. Consequently when mums say their baby is a slow feeder or hungry my eye brows disappear into my hairline as I mutter to myself "Poor wee soul!"

The use of medium or large-holed teats is the main sign of wrong feeding accompanied with difficulty to wind the babe and obtain a regular feeding routine.

The remainder of the results are dealt with under their appropriate headings. If in doubt, start at the beginning of Cries of a Baby (Nos 22-32) and work through to make sure, and also to find out where you are going wrong.

It is preferable to under-feed a baby in the process of getting organised. One can always give more food but one cannot retrieve what has already been given.

This article on the Results of Wrong Feeding is only a counter-check to make sure that everything is under control.

§

50

SLOW FEEDING

1. The feed should be given in 20 minutes SUCKING time.
2. Once the baby achieves the rhythm of bringing up wind without delay the babe should be fed and winded in 30 minutes.
3. If a medium-holed teat has been used the food is too thick. That is the dried milk has not been measured correctly or too little water has been used.
4. Should the total feeding period exceed $1/2$ hour or 35 minutes using a small-holed teat; the feed is too thick.
5. Demand feeding.

So many mothers have this problem which monopolises the whole day. Nothing gets done in the way of household chores. Result: Chaos; an overtired mother; unnecessary changing of food, all with the same result; neglect of other children and husband AND a crying baby into the bargain!

All the previous advice, if followed, eliminates this problem.

A slow feeder ALWAYS means something WRONG with the feeding. Very rarely is it the baby – unless, PERHAPS, handicapped. ALL THE MORE IMPORTANT TO CHECK YOUR FACTS AND METHODS.

51

WINDING

1. This is just as painful as colic so must not be ignored.
2. Do not accept this condition as "One of these things".
3. Examine carefully the methods of feeding and adjust accordingly.
4. It takes 36 to 48 hours to alter a winding rhythm especially when previously fed on a thick food.
5. To start with wind very frequently, (every 1/2 oz (1.5 cls) of food) with or without results.
6. When the problem had been overcome winding can be twice during a feed and once afterwards.
7. Patience is essential at the beginning.

It takes approximately 36 to 48 hours to alter a baby's rhythm of winding. During this period winding gradually becomes a faster process.

The majority of mothers have their husband, parent or relative to help them settle down with their new baby. To alter a baby's winding rhythm may mean taking an hour for one feed. Do not worry; leave everything else and have patience while you have help.

The ideal winding rhythm at the beginning is after every 1/2 oz (1.5 cls) of food. This prevents vomiting and possetting and so saves washing and ironing.

Within a few days of birth a mother knows when her babe has wind during a feed. When beginning this rhythm do not be surprised if there is a screaming session after the first 1/2 oz (1.5 cls). When crying no wind is brought up. Use your discretion; do not leave the baby crying too long at the beginning of the feed.

After the 36 or 48 hours even the first 1/2 oz (1.5 cls) the babe will cease to cry. Feeding stopped, up pops the wind, no trouble.

Once correct feeding has been established the baby can be winded less frequently, twice during the feed and at the end, but the more food that is given without winding, the longer it takes to wind. The actual feed takes the same length of time to give as usual.

Do not forget to use a small-holed teat.

DO NOT IGNORE this condition. The pain is as severe as colic.

Frequently lifting the baby between feeds to wind him is not good either for mother or the babe. The babe should remain relaxed between feeds not suffering from discomfort. The mother should be free to do whatever she wishes without interruptions.

§

52

STRONG URINE

CAUSES

1. Lack of water.
2. Wrong Feeding.
3. Solids too early.
4. Too much sugar intake, food or drink.
5. High temperature due to illness.

The first sign of strong urine is the smell of ammonia from the wet overnight nappy. Even at a very young age THE ONLY LEGITIMATE CAUSE is the high temperature during illness and even this can be rectified by giving more water to drink.

Teething is so often given as a cause. I say it is an excuse as it is not a real cause. The real causes are from number 1-4 of the Notes and they are always combined. Teething only aggravates the causes 1-4. Refer to feeding according to the age of the child.

Strong urine causes redness and even blistering, this causes sore buttocks and is accompanied with pain. Result; a crying baby.

Ointments may prevent the soreness from getting worse, it may partially improve the condition for a time, but IT WILL NOT CURE until the cause has been removed. Once the cause has been removed ointment is not necessary but it does help. Vaseline is very effective.

53

SORE BUTTOCKS

CAUSES

1. Strong Urine.
2. Too much sugar intake, food or drink.
3. Lack of water.
4. Constipation.
5. Too much or too strong an aperient (opening medicine).
6. Extra strong washing powders. All washing powders are stronger than soap flakes.
7. "Off the shelf" water softeners, (powder or liquid).
8. Fabric softeners.
9. Leaving the baby wet or soiled for long periods.
10. Failing to wash buttocks with soap and water or cleanse with oil before putting on clean nappy.
11. Gastro-enteritis.

This can cause a severe problem in spite of using various and expensive preparations to try and heal the skin. All this is a waste of money and time unless the cause or causes are removed. In all probability the mother and babe haunt the surgery and are ultimately referred to Out patients.

Work systematically through the causes. What to do about each cause is dealt with elsewhere in this book. Once the cause or causes are removed there will be a marked improvement in the condition from day to day. EXTRA STRICT HYGIENE IS ESSENTIAL DURING THIS PERIOD. Not only to prevent infection but to ease the pain and the discomfort of the baby.

DO NOT IGNORE THE SLIGHTEST SIGN OF SORE BUT-TOCKS. There is pain and discomfort from the earliest stage.

Detailed clothes washing instructions are given under Rashes (Nos 59-62).

Gastro-enteritis is very serious. The stools have a pungent smell. This condition is very serious. READ the appropriate article. (No 55), and ACT.

CONSTIPATION

CAUSES

1. Lack of water.
2. Wrong feeding, see Results of Wrong Feeding (No 49).
3. Solids too early.
4. Under-feeding (No 27).

A baby's stool should be yellow and have the consistency of freshly mixed mustard. The toddler's stool is soft but formed.

When a baby's stool "peels" off the nappy the baby is constipated. When solid, constipation is definitely due to lack of water– the baby is quenching his thirst on milk and there is also possetting (an acid-smelling regurgitation).

To overcome the immediate difficulty in a young babe pour into a medicine glass of Milk of Magnesia add some boiled water and mix. Give a portion of this mixture with each feed, (before, after or mixed with each feed). This prevents the pain and discomfort which can be caused by giving too much at one time. Repeat in the same manner the next day if necessary. This depends on the degree of the constipation – correctly fed: No constipation.

An older babe, approximately four months old, may be given prune juice or the juice of any dried fruit. Fresh orange juice may also be given, repeat several times a day.

Extra sugar or the use of brown sugar may overcome the difficulty but this is treating the effect and not the cause.

The giving of vitamin C drinks can disguise the fact that constipation is present. Due to the high sugar content of some of these products they act in the same way as the addition of extra sugar in the feed. The sugar acts as an irritant in the bowel, producing bowel movement. This produces other complications to cause anxiety. Refer to Sore Buttocks (No 53).

It is possible for 36 hours to pass before a baby's stool returns to normal, depending on the degree of constipation and the length of time the babe has suffered from this condition.

Remember! NEVER make medicine the daily food – TREAT the cause instead. Refer to Feeding or Weaning according to age.

§

55

GASTRO-ENTERITIS

1. VIOLENT green diarrhoea.
2. Foul, smelly, slimy stools.
3. Excessive loss of weight, for example up to 1/2 lb (226 g) per day.
4. Sore buttocks, starting from the back and spreading rapidly to the whole genital area. Read Sore Buttocks (No 53).
5. Crying, ill baby.
6. Pulling up of knees with cramping abdominal pain.
7. Vomiting at a later stage.
8. If untreated – DEATH.

Several mothers have requested that I should write about this serious condition. Before I do so, I say DO NOT be worried about the odd scanty green stool. It may be due to anything but NOT and I REPEAT, NOT gastro-enteritis.

Once a baby becomes infected with this condition there is no mistaking it, even if you have not seen it before. The violent diarrhoea, consisting of a foul smelling slimy stool, raises one's suspicions, accompanied by the rapid loss of weight. Depending on the severity of the attack depends the weight loss and no mother can miss that.

Vomiting is the last thing to rear its head. Then the condition is serious. IMMEDIATE help is vital. Even while you are getting help, a 1/2 oz (1.5 cls) or more of water MUST be given EVERY 1/2 hour, given a few drops at a time otherwise the baby will vomit and aggravate the condition. This is to replace the fluid lost by the diarrhoea. In fact 1 oz (3.0 cls) per 1/2 hour should be given FROM THE BEGINNING before vomiting commences.

This is one reason I discourage the giving of sugary "Off the Shelf" vitamin drinks. So many mothers flavour all water given with these products. SUGAR ACTS AS AN IRRITANT to the bowel and so aggravates diarrhoea with drastic results. Babies drinking this flavoured water usually refuse plain boiled water and you cannot struggle with an ill baby! BUT IT CAN DIE due to lack of plain water!

Gastro-enteritis is spread mainly by blue-bottles and flies. In about 1948/1949 insecticides were made available to the general public. their regular use gradually reduced the fly population to a minimum. Waste food matter was burnt on open fires. Today there are few open fires owing to central heating. Unwrapped and inadequately wrapped waste food is left in the dustbins! An ideal breeding ground for flies! Do not forget that flies and blue-bottles, through time, have become immune to insecticides.

DO GET ADVICE EARLY if in doubt. Any Health Visitor will confirm the condition or put your mind at ease if your GP is not available.

In the remote Highlands and Islands where a doctor is not always available your District Nurse or Health Visitor may advise castor oil. Do not be alarmed, she will state the dose. NEVER give the oil WITHOUT professional advice. It is an old-fashioned effective remedy. It increases the diarrhoea for a few hours. This scourges the bowel of the infection and then the diarrhoea ceases. Plenty of boiled water and gradual increase of milk feeds puts your babe on the road to recovery.

Just as a matter of interest; a babe in the Outer Hebrides was born $8^{1}/_{2}$ lb (5.5kg), approx., breast fed and gaining weight. Later, I was called in and the babe weighed approximately 2lb (under 1.0 kg – I did not weigh him). He was even vomitting water. The mother had taken him off the breast, substituted raw unrestrained cow's milk and had given the dried milk to the calf. The baby was suffering from gastro-enteritus and was literally dying. I eventually got him onto the right road, though it took a long time and many hours of supervision with no hospital available. The baby is now a grown man and as strong as an ox. He was the only boy in the family of five children.

56

PUERPERAL DEPRESSION

SOME CAUSES

1.   When a tired anxious mother becomes pregnant.
2.   A long and difficult labour.
3.   Feeding difficulties; Breast and artificial.
4.   Disturbed nights, night feeding.
5.   Unhelpful, demanding husband.
6.   Insufficient knowledge and advice to cope with a crying baby plus an awkward toddler.
7.   Un-disciplined, disruptive family.
8.   When a mother becomes pregnant with the hope of saving the marriage.
9.   An illegitimate pregnancy.
10. Attending to an elderly or sick relative.

Throughout this book the advice given has been to avoid Puerperal Depression; a soul-destroying complaint with far reaching effects depending on its severity. Very little constructive advice or treatment is given for this mental state and, worse still, the condition need never arise.

In spite of the usual advice given, mothers have requested me to write an article on this subject. They wish for further information in order to make sure they know EXACTLY what the condition is, how to recognise the early symptoms and more important, what to do about it.

The causes are varied, but all are triggered off by one or more of the causes listed; Nos 3 and 4 are the most common. These result in the mother losing 14 hours sleep per week! Refer to *How to Cut Out Night Feeding* (No 47). This, of course, means a tired mother, a crying baby with irregular feeds which cuts down still further relaxation time. In spite of her efforts and her husband's to pacify the infant the mother is on the go all day.

Eventually she just sits down and literally sobs, clutching her crying baby or just leaving him screaming in the cot or on the settee. Should a solution not be found desperation point is reached and there could be a battered baby, even with kind, conscientious parents. Long term sedatives for the baby or the mother is NOT the answer.

The milder form of puerperal depression and the beginning of the more serious condition is recognised when the mother sleeps late in the morning and is not "mobile" until approximately 11.00 am. She copes until 7.00 pm then falls asleep in the chair. This is quite different from "Cat-napping" when after 10 to 20 minutes she shakes her feathers and is alive again. Her interest has gone regarding hobbies, TV, reading and conversation. Her husband, if helpful, will nurse the crying baby until feeding time.

At night the poor mother is unable to sleep – all the problems of the day and tomorrow come crowding in, demanding to be solved while waiting for sleep to take over. Then comes the full circle! She falls asleep, and is awakened by the crying babe DEMANDING TO BE FED. What a life!! Sex life becomes nil, bringing its own problems. This may lead, in some cases, to breakdown of the marriage.

To prevent this sad state of affairs, read this book CAREFULLY! contained in it are the answers. Refer to Infant Feeding (Nos 33-45) and follow the advice. Should you read this advice too late to prevent depression it is at least not too late to do something about it.

REFER TO THE ARTICLE ON STOUT (Nos 4-6). You did not get into this condition overnight. Depending on its duration and the number of children and so on it could take 18 months to 2 years before complete recovery.

Do not be despondent! After two weeks you will feel the beneficial results of the stout! Believe it or not AFTER two weeks of taking stout daily I can look at a mother and, without asking questions, KNOW whether she has followed my advice! BUT YOU ARE NOT THROUGH THE WOOD YET. Continue to take the stout for an extra three months for every child you already have.

57

BATTERED BABIES

1. A baby continually crying.
2. An overtired mother.
3. Puerperal depression.
4. Mental illness and subnormality.
5. A very intelligent husband.
6. Poor housing conditions.
7. Basic neglect; wishing the death of a baby.

A great deal has been written and spoken about the battered baby. I have endeavoured to put the reasons in order of priority.

A baby crying continually is a potential battered baby! The mother gets no relaxation because of anxiety, trying everything to quieten him to no avail. meals are not ready, the baby cries all the evening and, of course without fail, is fed during the night. The poor mother or father is up half the night nursing the babe, taking it in turns to allow each other and the other children some rest. Overtired parents, because of frustration at getting no results, become short tempered and begin shouting at each other. Sooner rather than later; depression, and a battered baby. Often the hope that the baby will die and relieve mother (usually single) of moral responsibility.

If I had a baby crying like this, and a Health Visitor, Midwife or Family Doctor came into my home and Said "He is a baby who needs very little sleep" (and that is often said!) I would feel like throwing something at them!

I have listed the reasons for a baby crying. (Nos 22-32). Follow ALL the instructions, and you will find the answer. When the cause is removed the baby will quieten.

A baby crying in this manner is the equivalent to an adult shouting his head off! It is hard work, tiring, hot and uncomfortable.

Puerperal depression due to overtiredness and anaemia is, in this day and age, a disgrace to anyone having a mother and child in their care.

Mental illness, (including puerperal depression), and subnormality are the only legitimate reasons for battering because the individuals have not full control of their faculties. A quiet, contented baby cuts down the risk, even in these cases.

As a rule the husbands or boy friends are less tolerant than the mothers towards crying babies. ESPECIALLY when the relationship is unstable. These men are inclined to be unco-operative and unsympathetic: "I'll give that baby something to cry for!" Hence cigarette burns, broken limbs and so on. Of course the babe continues to cry vigorously but it gives the "Batterer" (whether male or female) the satisfaction of relieving their tension.

Bad housing conditions make bad – worse! But a quiet contented baby rules out this reason. No normal person will batter a happy, contented baby. He is UNDEMANDING and happy.

Basic neglect, of course, is a criminal offence no matter what the reason. The neglect may result from parents who are driven to this as a way out to rid them of a persistently crying baby, or a discontented toddler or child. In all cases a poor sleeper, resulting in disturbed nights.

The answer is, follow ALL my advice, read the chapter Puerperal Depression, (No 56). A subject requested by mothers.

COT DEATHS

1. The use of pillows – Smothering.
2. Baby lying on his back – Swallowing vomit, Choking.
3. Lying on their tummies – Smothering.
4. Crying babies being taken into parents' bed. – Overlaying – Smothering.
5. Feeding a baby during the night in bed – Smothering, Choking.
6. Overweight – See Nos 26 and 39. – Hampered movement.
7. Hypothermia or over heating – see No 25.
8. Some medical conditions such as Virus Pneumonia.

Many mothers have asked me to write on this subject which causes so much heart break when it happens.

In this day and age not many mothers use pillows in the cots. Sometimes they use them in prams to prop up the older babies. Providing the pillows are hard and firm there is little or no danger except when used in the cot or pram for sleeping.

ALWAYS lie your baby on his side even if you must use a pillow at his back to keep him in position. Should the baby vomit it can drain out of his mouth and not impair breathing. Lying on his back he can breathe the vomit into his lungs and so suffocate himself. Providing a baby is fed and winded correctly, this will not happen, but it is better to be safe than sorry!

How often a crying baby is taken into the parents' bed FOR PEACE and the baby is smothered. The baby quietens and the parents fall off to sleep, turn over onto the baby and smother him.

I have known bad housing conditions where there has been no place to put the new baby but in the parents' bed. So be it! A STRONG cardboard carton or drawer is ESSENTIAL and use it as a cot. A baby was smothered under these circumstances because the parents failed to take my advice. I had even procured a drawer from another family to use as a cot but the parents refused to use it. The baby was smothered when 16 days old. Providing the baby has his own box or drawer placed across the top of the bed, he is safe.

Night feeding is another common cause, especially with breast fed babies. So easy to take the baby into bed and a tired mother falls asleep. It can also happen with bottle feeding. Another reason for my not liking night feeding.

Overweight: refer to Over-feeding (No 26) and Weight Gain during the First Year of Life (No 39). This is a very common cause of cot deaths for the babe's movements are impaired similar to those of an obese adult.

Hypothermia has been dealt with earlier in this book (No 25). This can happen especially amongst immigrant communities where landlords do not provide heating for their tenants, not even for the cooking! The baby just "Sleeps Away".

In the motoring age I must mention the baby left in a shut up car standing for a length of time in the hot sun while the family go shopping or have a meal.

The medical condition virus pneumonia USED TO BE KNOWN AS SILENT PNEUMONIA. Unlike a child with bronchitis who is fractious, the babe lies very quiet as if asleep but the nostrils move excessively with each intake of breath. Food is quietly refused. Medical aid is required immediately. DEMAND A HOME VISIT FROM THE DOC-TOR.

There are some other medical conditions which can be the cause of death but the parents cannot be held responsible for these reasons.

FACE AND BODY RASHES

59

GENERAL

CAUSES

1. Some washing powders
2. "Off the Shelf" water softeners – powder or liquid.
3. Some fabric softeners.
4. Some soap flakes.
5. Some perfumed toilet soap.
6. The rashes are aggravated by the warm weather.

How many times have you observed a baby with unusually red cheeks and wondered why! Should the skin surface appear taut and smooth like tissue paper it is brought on by the listed causes. During warm weather this may be accompanied by a raised rash, caused also by the listed causes.

Various prepared washing aids contain strong chemicals varying in degrees according to the manufacturer's formula. The hard water fails to remove the chemicals during rinsing.

There is always a varied amount of perspiration from the body, depending on the amount of clothing and the surrounding atmosphere. The chemicals remaining in the bedding and the personal clothes react on this perspiration, causing the rash. If ignored it can culminate in extensive eczema. A babe of five months old developed extensive eczema on the face and body. Immediately I said "Fabric Softener". Correct! Once all the clothes and bedding were washed in soap flakes ONLY, the eczema improved and was soon cured.

I have known a facial rash caused by the use of soapflakes manufactured by one firm which obviously contained chemicals, while those produced by another firm were perfectly safe.

I have written an article on the Washing of clothes (No 61) in this chapter. I feel sure you will find it helpful and I hope it will make life a little easier for those concerned.

PINK'S DISEASE

1. A rare disease.
2. Restricted to coal mining areas.
3. Distressing condition.
4. The child fails "To Thrive".
5. Cross between measles and under-feeding.
6. No cure. Disease takes its own time.
7. Difficult to diagnose.

I have worked in the North-East of England in areas of the deep pits and became familiar with Pink's Disease. I have decided to include the condition in this book.

The disease is so closely connected with under-feeding and because of its rarity, it is difficult to diagnose.

Coal mining today is practically obsolete but given time it will turn the full circle and return.

Pink's Disease is UNIQUE to the coal mining areas. It is supposed to be caused, and I am sure it is, by the released gasses and dust from the smouldering slag tips of the DEEP PITS. The babies who suffered from the disease resided within a certain area and mileage in the path of the prevailing winds blowing from the deep pit slag tips.

The babies appear to be "Wasting Away". This is correct in so much that there is failure to gain weight and they look THOROUGHLY MISERABLE. The red eyes and face accompany the CONTINUED half hearted cry, which persists throughout the 24 hours. The condition resembles a cross between measles and under-feeding. NOTHING ALLAYS this crying. The parents and baby suffer from lack of sleep and relaxation and all become frustrated.

The condition is so closely associated with under-feeding that "Feeding Up" the baby is the automatic reflex but to no avail. Investigations carried out are also to no avail to helping the diagnosis and treatment. THERE IS NO TREATMENT.

Clock Feeding (No 46), helps to cope with the condition and does help the diagnosis.

Again I stress there is no cure for this disease apart from time and patience. The condition lasts for several weeks, depending on the severity. IT IS NOT FATAL.

Apart from time and patience it is ESSENTIAL to continue with Clock Feeding (No 46) and drinks of water. The babe must be kept warm but not *Too Hot* (No 23).

Recovery leaves no ill-effects on the baby but it does leave the parents very tired.

§

61

WASHING CLOTHES

AVOID

1. Strong washing powder.
2. "Off the shelf" water softeners – liquid or powder.
3. Fabric softeners also washing powders with softeners.
4. Certain brands of soap flakes.

Should a young baby or child have a rash on their cheeks, around the neck or on their body suspect one of the four reasons. Ointment may soothe but only keeps the rash at bay. Once the ointment is discontinued the condition reverts to its untreated state.

The elderly usually have their rash on their back. The back is the warmest part of their body; sitting in a chair and resting against warm cushions causes extra perspiration which reacts on the chemicals left in the clothes after rinsing (hard water). This creates a problem. Often the elderly live on their own. Applying ointment to the back is virtually impossible. Therefore it is essential to avoid the cause.

This rash causes tenderness and irritation to both young and old alike.

SOAP JELLY

Grate a well known brand of green kitchen soap. Add water to cover and heat until dissolved. The final consistency should be that of washing up liquid. Add more water to achieve this. This makes it ready for immediate use. It is cheaper than soap flakes. It will keep indefinitely so it may be made in large quantities.

Reading the "Avoids" it appears that no clothes ought to be washed at all, but this is not the case. As I have said before, babies' skins vary in texture but clothes do require washing and STAINS REQUIRE REMOVING and WITHOUT skin rashes.

Stained clothes, sheets, bibs, nappies and so on MUST be washed in the washing machine using a MILD SOAP POWDER. Complete the full washing cycle. THIS IS FOLLOWED by a full washing cycle using soap flakes or jelly. There is no need to be extravagant with the flakes or jelly as the clothes are already clean. IT IS ESSENTIAL to remove the chemical left in the clothes. Only a small quantity is required. AGAIN I SAY: DO NOT USE FABRIC SOFTENER AFTER THIS. YOU WILL BE BACK TO SQUARE ONE.

Before I finish I add – Should you have no problems with your babe's skin just continue with your own routine.

THUMB SUCKING

63

PREVENTION

1. Stop this BEFORE it becomes a habit.
2. Swaddle the baby from birth or splint the arm using $1/3$ of a $2^1/2$ inch crepe bandage.
3. If the habit has already been formed break VERY GRADUALLY.
4. Refer to Persistent Sucking (No 64).

Before birth the baby's hands were in close proximity to his mouth. A baby has not yet acquired the art of associating hands with the mouth but the faithful thumb wanders nevertheless. Babies are opportunists and plus the strong sucking instinct, begin the thumb sucking habit, if not stopped immediately, within days of birth.

The prevention at birth is simple. Swaddle the baby; wrapping a shawl around the baby including the arms. This obviously prevents the hands reaching the mouth and gives a feeling of comfort and security during the early days of life. Swaddling is considered "old hat" but when the weather is very frosty or windy, depending on what part of the country you live in, mittens are not sufficient when outside to keep a young baby's hands warm. Swaddling is the answer. In more temperate climes (such as cosy Surrey) the crepe bandage splint is adequate.

The first time you find your baby with the thumb in his mouth do not hesitate, gently remove it. Watch him for a while, especially when he is falling asleep, in case it returns.

PERSISTENT THUMB SUCKING

This includes: fingers/thumb, dummy (comforter) and bottle sucking.

CAUSING

1. Permanent damage to the bone structure of the mouth.
2. Adenoids due to incorrect breathing (mouth breathing).
3. Teeth may not grow in the correct position for chewing and biting.
4. Poor diet, sweet eating, chewing of gum and smoking in later life.
5. (Can cause) Digestive disorders in adult life.
6. (Can cause) Embarrassment to parents and children.

TO PREVENT THUMB SUCKING

1. It is ideal to prevent the habit forming at birth.
2. When cuddling the baby play with the guilty hand.
3. When older splint elbow joint by applying a wide crepe bandage. Use approximately 1/3.
4. Leave the splint on for short periods of three to four hours and during the night when asleep.

65

HOW TO CURE PERSISTENT THUMB SUCKING

1. Keep the child under close observation.
2. Splint the elbow joint by applying the bandage to the bare arm or over the sleeve or coat if playing outside.
3. Apply the splint regularly.
4. Keep the child active, particularly the hands.
5. NEVER frustrate the child.
6. Win the child's co-operation.
7. Be prepared for periodic lapses.
8. DO NOT punish the child.

A bad habit is so called because a simple action is allowed to develop without restraint and is capable of causing mental or physical damage to the individual. The forming of a bad habit has a simple beginning governed by the force of circumstances.

The older baby or child presents a different problem to that of a very young baby, primarily because the habit is well established. The older the child – the longer the time it takes to cure. In fact there is no limit.

Persistent thumb sucking includes fingers, dummies and teats of feeding bottles. I have seen a teat used without being attached to a bottle. This is a very dangerous habit! Sucking over a long period may damage the bony structure of the mouth and the set of the teeth perhaps requiring a brace in later life. The thumb is the worst offender.

Persistent thumb sucking demands mouth breathing. Adenoids develop. To demonstrate this try holding your nose and chewing hard foods such as raw vegetables, meat or apples and see how you manage. Repeatedly you stop to mouth breathe. For a child this mouth breathing may continue for a while but it will ultimately result in the consumption of soft sugary foods for ease and convenience. This poor diet combined with mouth breathing accelerates chest infection and adenoids.

Left unchecked the sucking instance does not disappear. The child becomes a sweet eater. Early in adult life sweet eating continues also gum chewing and smoking (especially chain smoking). This replaces the thumb. Even nail biting cannot be ignored.

The persistent sucker includes the age group from three months to six years (even older). The most satisfactory way to cope is to direct the child's attention and keep both hands occupied. Ball games, constructive games etc. I appreciate you are unable to devote all your time to this activity. Splinting of the arm is called for. The most satisfactory way is to use a broad crepe bandage. This is not cruel!! It allows full movement of the hand and shoulder. This method is useful when you are carrying out household chores.

Avoid frustration especially with the older child. Various mixtures such as mustard or bitter alloes are sometimes used on the fingers but to no avail. Win over the co-operation of the child. Splint for short periods but often.

NEVER, NEVER resort to punishment in any form. It is capable of causing many other problems.

Appreciate the fact it is NOT the child's fault he is a persistent sucker – IT IS YOURS.

EASY TO PREVENT —- SO DIFFICULT TO CURE!!!

POTTY TRAINING

66

THE BEGINNING

1. Commence soon after birth.
2. Clock Feeding (No 46), simplifies the training. The bowels and bladder act approximately at the same hour each day according to feeding times.
3. Children can be clean and dry during the day by one year old, and during the night by 18 months old.
4. Commence serious training after full weaning is completed at 6½ months.
5. When the times are established, pot the child 5-10 minutes beforehand.
6. Get the child used to using toilets from a very early age. Hold the child over the toilet, even if no urine is passed. The babe will get used to being there.

At the beginning it is the baby training the mother! So be it! The mother's task is made easier when her child, due to Clock Feeding, has a bowel movement and passes urine at regular intervals. This DEPENDS ENTIRELY on the feeding and weaning instructions being STRICTLY ADHERED TO, plus the drinks of water given at the same time between meals.

Mothers tell me their babies pass urine 5-10 minutes after the drink of water or feed. This information may help you. Within 2-3 days of close observation, mother and child have the technique off to a fine art.

Bowel movements must be soft and formed, not peeling off the nappies passed at regular intervals, (once or twice a day). This depends on regular meals, regular drinks of water and the fruit and vegetables given at each meal. Refer to *Fruit and Vegetables for Weaning* (Nos 77, 78).

It has been the mothers themselves who have informed me as to the age when their children are dry during the day and night. It can be as young as 9 months during the day and 14 months at night.

I mention the fact of getting the child used to the ordinary toilet from the beginning; It does save screams and yells of fear when the child is older.

§

67

POTTY TANTRUMS

CAUSES

1. Strong Urine.
2. Constipation.
3. Loose stools or diarrhoea.
4. An excess of wrong feeding.
5. Wanting attention.

How much rubbish has been spoken, written and advised on this subject – and to no avail! Psychological reasons have been given: *the mother is not giving enough attention to the child*; *the child is demanding too much attention*; *there is jealousy of the new baby*; *he will grow out of it!!* Had anyone given me this advice, in desperation I would have thrown something at them. And handed over the child concerned!! (figuratively speaking).

Potty tantrums are due SOLELY TO WRONG FEEDING AND NOTHING ELSE!! No matter what you think! The causes: strong urine, constipation and loose stools are the result of wrong feeding.

The main disrupting cause is milk, milky food and sugary drinks. Refer to *Milk, Weaning* (Nos 68-80) – regardless of age – and vitamin drinks. The urine becomes strong, the genitals, as a result, become inflamed and sore. A girl when on the potty, has the genitals exposed to the strong urine flowing over them, causing pain. The natural reaction is to throw a tantrum or, if forced to sit, not to use the potty and shortly afterwards wet her pants. Mothers nearly go berserk. The child when standing, causes the urine to flow directly downwards instead of flowing over the sore genitals. It is still painful but less so than when sitting.

In the case of the boy this is not so obvious. It is the inside of the penis and the tip which is affected. The result is the same. Sitting on the potty causes pain.

When constipated, the anus (back passage), is stretched and painful. Sitting on the potty the anus is stretched even more, the very sitting position cuts out muscular control. This causes pain, the amount depending on the severity of the constipation. The anal skin can be broken a nick). The pain has to be experienced to be appreciated. Children are no fools! Standing up, soiling pants or nappies is less painful as there is some muscular control present. Do not blame the children. Follow the full weaning diet using the dried fruits etc. to overcome the constipation.

This problem can continue until 6 years if the correct advice is not given or not followed.

Loose stools or diarrhoea (not gastro-enteritis) are primarily caused by milky foods and too much sugary vitamin drinks and so on. Unless these are cut out completely no satisfactory results will be obtained.

Once the child realises that bowel movements and the passing of urine are no longer painful, you will get results.

THE ADVANTAGES OF MILK BEFORE THE AGE OF SIX MONTHS

1. Milk under the age of six months is the natural food.
2. Because it is the natural food it is VERY IMPORTANT dried milk is measured carefully. Refer to How to Measure Dried Milk (Nos 41-42).
3. Milk alone during this period is essential as it does not upset Nature's balance of food necessary for the baby.
4. Providing sufficient water is given the birth weight is EXACT LY double by the age of six months.
5. Regardless of the birth weight of the baby milk alone is required but it must be given according to the birth weight throughout the six months.

When a baby is born there is only sufficient fat on his body to make the birth easy, if it can be called easy! But this covering of fat is not adequate to keep the baby warm. Milk with its high content of fat and sugar doubles the birth weight in six months. The giving of sugary "Off the Shelf" vitamin drinks plus the giving of solids under the age of six months upsets this balance. These items are responsible for an excessive weight gain, with accompanying complications.

The actual "Growth" (bone and muscle building) during this period of six months is negligible in comparison to the laying down of fat. The small amount of protein content in the milk is sufficient to repair the wear and tear of breathing, crying and kicking. The remainder is used for the small amount of growth.

THE DISADVANTAGES OF MILK AFTER
THE AGE OF SIX MONTHS

1. Overweight.
2. 2-hourly routine.
3. Possetting – what some call "Happy Vomiting". It has a vile, acid smell, caused by an over-full stomach. Result: a great deal of extra washing, ironing and dry cleaning.
4. An excessive consumption of "Off the Shelf" sugary drinks.
5. Prolonged period of enuresis (bed wetting).
6. Frequent colds, bronchitis and teething problems.
7. Behaviour problems.
8. Poor appetite.
9. Wakeful nights.
10. Dental caries (decayed teeth) in later life.

After the age of six months the baby is no longer a baby but a "Baby Toddler". He is not content to lie passively in the cot or the pram. He learns to play with toys, crawl, pull himself up and eventually walk. At the end of six months milk is no longer required. It is too bulky and has too high a fat content.

This increased activity activates an unbelievable amount of bone and muscle building with the equivalent amount of wear and tear. To ensure the child remains happy and contented during this strenuous period, milk MUST BE REPLACED by the CONCENTRATED PROTEINS: meat, fish, eggs and cheese. These foods contain all the requirements for a growing body, with a compliment of vegetables and fruit.

ESKIMO children, once they are weaned, no longer drink milk. It is in too short supply!! Because of the harsh climate they are weaned some months later. They are too young to cope with the rich seal fat. The milk covers the transitional period. After weaning the food is seal, reindeer and fish. These foods contain everything required, including the extra fat, complimented with wild berries that grow during the short Summer Season. The amount of calcium and other body building properties in these concentrated proteins certainly produce strong hardy people and certainly people with the strongest teeth in the world.

In this day and age how many times does one hear "The child must have its pint of milk daily". I hear it repeated and repeated. Today no one really knows why this phrase is repeated. Various reasons are given but, I am afraid, not the real reason.

I hear that phrase echoing and re-echoing into the distant past of over 70 years; as far back as the Coal and General Strike of 1926 followed by the years of depression. No one, I may add, who has not lived through that period has any idea what the word Depression means! Children were LITERALLY walking skeletons, underweight, under-fed and inadequately clothed. EVEN to the tune of ONE garment (and that had been cut down and was thin and worn). They ran about bare-foot in all the snow and slush. Their legs frostbitten, with running, broken chilblains! CAN YOU IMAGINE IT? – In the bitter Northern Winters. IT WAS DURING THIS PERIOD THAT MILK BECAME MORE IMPORTANT THAN MEAT. MILK DRINKING WAS THE ONLY WAY TO COVER THEIR POOR STARVED BODIES WITH FAT TO KEEP THEM WARM. After they had regained their weight protein ought to have been their dominant food, but World War II broke out. Many children were still under-nourished and rationing made meat, fish, eggs and cheese scarce. The pint of milk per child continued. It was essential.

Today in Britain no child, unless deliberately deprived, is half starved. The majority of children are overfed because of excessive milk drinking and early weaning – and LACK OF WATER TO DRINK!!

Milk, in this country, is no longer an essential food for children. The years when it was vital have passed into history, and I hope for ever!

IMPORTANT POINTS REGARDING WEANING

1. DO NOT COMMENCE WEANING BEFORE THE AGE OF SIX MONTHS.
2. Prepare each item of food in quantity, catering for three meals of that particular food.
3. THE THEME IS SOLIDS, WATER, MILK.
4. Do NOT be afraid to CUT OUT MILK.
5. Water MUST be given with meals and between meals.
6. Do not underestimate a child's appetite.
7. DO NOT WASTE FOOD. Use your fridge and freezer – this is why you purchased them.
8. An adequate amount of protein guarantees undisturbed nights and even during teething.
9. EVENTUALLY, (within a space of two weeks), a five-hour interval between meals is established and milk is completely cut out.
10. NEVER give cooked cheese. It goes tough. Add grated cheese to COOKED food.
11. DO NOT USE A LIQUIDISER for protein foods. They must be of a uniform chewing consistency.
12. Mince protein foods AFTER cooking on a FINE CUTTER of a household mincer.
13. Cooked dried fruits may be liquidised, using their own juice.
14. AVOID cereals, pasta, custard, vitamin drinks, squashes, yoghurt, bread etc. in ANY FORM.
15. The child will be three times his birth weight at one year old.
16. Allow the child to be the judge of HOW MUCH protein he requires.
17. The amount of protein required depends on weather, activity and environment. This means the appetite will vary with each meal.
18. Give dried fruit as a second course, WITHOUT custard. If very sour it may be sweetened with CLOVER honey. The fruit may be liquidised in its own juice.

19. NEVER GIVE potatoes or bananas listed in No 14; they are too bulky.
20. As the intake of protein increases so the milk is automatically cut down – and FINALLY REFUSED – within a period of two weeks.
21. When visiting take the child's food with you.

I repeat, do not commence weaning before six months. Had you found it necessary to do so then something has gone wrong with the feeding during the first six months of life. The usual reason is colic. Or at four to five months "The milk was no longer satisfying the babe!" Should you have failed to give more than 8 oz of milk for a feed, in some instances more is required. Of course the babe is not satisfied with the milk. It is not the milk at fault but the quantity. Remember a baby 10 lb at birth requires 10 oz of milk per feed (28.0 cls) when six months old. that is TWICE as much as a babe of 5 lb (2.3 kg) birthweight.

From the age of six weeks WATER should be given BETWEEN feeds to keep the milk drinking under control.

It is strange how many involved in Child Care are so eager to advise the introduction of solids at a very early age instead of advising more milk. This early introduction of solids completely upsets the babe by more than doubling his birthweight by the age of six months and causing overweight. When the child should be eating "Solids" protein three times a day he is stuffed with cereals – cereals used to thicken foods and rusks – and, of course quantities of milk. Rusks are ONLY 1930's bread and milk done up in a fancy pack and sold at fancy prices!! All this pappy food, whether sweet or savoury, requires 1–2 pints (57–114 cls) of milk per day; 6-12 pints (341–682 cls) THE EQUIVALENT FOR AN ADULT! according to their weight. "My baby is a drinker. Every lump in his food he spits out!" CAN YOU BLAME HIM? Could you, as an adult, drink all that milk per day *and* eat normal FOOD? No, of course you couldn't! You would eat biscuits and cakes. they are easily eaten and digested. Do you now appreciate why these children suffer from repeated coughs, colds, bronchitis and disturbed sleep?

When preparing family meals prepare three meals of meat, fish, eggs and cheese. Total 12 meals. Choose from "Lists of Foods" (Nos 75-78). After all he MUST have three dinners a day in order to consume the adequate amount of protein. The same applies to the dried fruits (12 meals). This saves fiddling around; the child is independent of family meals, snacks during the day and unsuitable meals at unsuitable times. The meals must be HEATED THOROUGHLY in a heat-resistant pudding basin placed in a pan of water, a steamer, pressure cooker or micro wave. The food may be given cold.

A good idea is to take prepared food with you when visiting. This prevents you commandeering the kitchen when your hostess is trying to prepare a meal.

Allow the child to be the judge of the amount of protein. The amounts vary from meal to meal, depending on environment and activity. One child of eight months was sitting in his pram outside. Snow was on the ground and a cold wind was blowing. He came in for his dinner and he ATE ½ lb (227 g) of MEAT! I can see you holding your hands up in horror. Refer back to the Eskimos! Think of the quantity of meat and fish they eat because of the cold! The same happened with the eight month old child. He used that quantity of food in keeping warm.

The five-hour intervals between meals is essential. The protein takes five hours to digest. By all means give a meal after five hours but NOT before. The child can usually wait.

Weaning should be so easy! and during the following months there should be no problems. How many mothers can honestly say this is so? Problems usually commence about eight months. A child begins waking at night, even for a drink of water. No matter what the reason, the parents lose sleep. The excuse is teething or whatever. THESE ARE NOT THE REASONS BUT THE LACK OF PROTEIN IS!!

A reminder; ensure the food is not sloppy but of a uniform chewing consistency. Don't liquidise it!

THE REQUIREMENTS FOR WEANING

1. A household mincer.
2. Containers to hold four different protein foods (prepared).
3. Containers to hold four different types of dried fruits. These will last for three days.
4. Steamer pudding basins in which to heat preferably in a pressure cooker or microwave, the prepared protein, vegetables and gravy.
5. Steamer pudding basins in which to cook in the same way the dried fruit.
6. An egg spoon, preferably bone. At the beginning use the rounded handle of a teaspoon.
7. A liquidiser to grind down casserole gravy and vegetable soups to use as gravy for the babe's food.
8. A liquidiser is also useful for emulsifying dried fruit.
9. Powdered gelatine to make jellies from liquidised fruit or fresh fruit juice. A change from the dried fruit. DO NOT use commercial table jellies as a substitute.

The whole idea of this article is to prevent you fiddling with small quantities of food. Fiddling with small quantities will, before long, mean you are giving the child what you are having and at the same time as you are having your meal. Having the child's food prepared in advance means you have your meal in peace at the time you have planned and you avoid a child niggling on because he is hungry and his food (yours) is not ready.

The household mincer is a MUST and should always be used until teething is completed at about 2 years. Then the food may be cut up. The six-month old child accepts FINELY minced food, saving the tedious job of using a food grinder.

There is no necessity to purchase expensive containers for heating food. A polystyrene pudding basin is suitable.

You require four larger containers for the four different proteins. Four containers for the four different kinds of fruits. It is not imperative you use heat resistant containers for this. You do require two heat resistant containers to heat up the maincourse and second course, (if necessary).

This information is to prevent you wasting your money on purchasing "Off the Shelf" prepared foods which are expensive and not necessary. On the consumption of animal protein depends whether the child is happy and contented or otherwise. By this I mean, visit your friend for a cup of tea and a chat. Instead of the child amusing himself he grizzles for attention. The child is into everything, pulling everything off the top! Result? No conversation, no enjoyment. We have all had, at some time or another, to cope with a child like this. All involved with such a child, including your friends, are relieved when the visit has come to an end. A very bad state of affairs! This is one cause of antagonism between parents and grand-parents. AND ALL BECAUSE OF LACK OF PROTEIN!!

To give you some idea as to how much protein a child can eat: At 6 1/2 months a child can eat two eggs at meal time; at 8 – 8 1/2 months, three to 3 1/2 eggs depending on environment and activity.

If a child can eat a whole apple or orange as "Pudding" it is a sure sign that too little protein has been given and the child could be restless during the next five hours or the subsequent ones. Besides, this amount of fruit consumed three times a day will cause loose stools. The mother, in desperation at coping with soiled nappies exclaims "I cannot follow your advice, the child has an allergy to fruit". THIS IS UNTRUE! The fruit is being used as bulk to make up for the deficiency of protein. IT IS IMPORTANT – only sufficient fruit must be given three times a day to maintain a soft regular bowel movement. Reduce the quantity when necessary but still three times a day.

The spoon used for weaning requires consideration, especially during the early days of the teething period. It is a good idea when solids are first introduced to use the rounded handle of a teaspoon, thus ensuring a very small quantity is given at a time. Direct the food into the side of the mouth. This helps the acceptance of solids and avoids the spitting out. By the time the child has manipulated the food that is swallowed. Boiled eggs are disliked intensely – it is like eating lumpy custard – ugh!!! The same goes for other foods; that means no surplus gravy.

ONLY enough to bind the food together into a chewing consistency. This method converts sucking into a chewing action.

Once solids are accepted an "Apostle" spoon may be used; a small spoon for a small mouth. The best spoon of all is one of the very old-fashioned bone egg-spoons. If obtainable!! Or a very small plastic spoon. There are no hard edges for tender gums.

Remember; a teaspoon for the babe is the equivalent of a table spoon for you and a cup is the same as a large crock pudding basin. This is why I stress Using a small spoon. Result? Clean feeding.

§

72

PROCESS OF WEANING

1. Solids, Water, Milk.
2. 7.00 – 8.00 am give as much protein and vegetables, hot or cold, as the child can eat.
3. Follow this with one or two teaspoonfuls of prepared fruit.
4. Then as much water as the child will take.
5. ONLY A SMALL breast or bottle feed will be necessary. Do not be concerned if this is refused.
6. Drink of water between meals.
7. Five hours after breakfast, dinner is given.
8. Repeat as for breakfast but differ the flavours.
9. Drink of water between meals.
10. Five hours after dinner give supper – repeat as for breakfast and dinner.
11. Later in the evening the babe may require a drink of water ONLY if he is awake. Discourage this.
12. As the protein intake increases so will the intake of milk decrease.
13. In the morning the babe may appreciate a drink of water before breakfast in addition to that taken during the meal.
14. If disturbed, to answer the door for instance, place the food well out of the child's reach.

At the age of six months the babe wakens approximately between 7.00 and 8.00 am. This is quite a suitable time to commence weaning. Unless, of course, it is in the middle of the family's breakfast time. One thing I do stress is DO NOT START the habit of giving a drink of milk or fruit juice to tide the babe over until breakfast. Give a drink of water by all means. GIVE AN EARLIER MEAL. This is one reason I disapprove of a 10.00 am breakfast.

It has been mentioned in this book five hours is a MUST between one meal and another. It may be over five hours but NEVER under. Within one week or less milk will not be required.

Food given in small mouthfuls using a rounded HANDLE of a teaspoon takes less time than giving the babe great mouthfuls of food which are difficult to chew and swallow.

I think the routine is self explanatory. Arrange the meals to suit the household routine. In other words do not allow the babe's meals to coincide with those of the household. One is not able to relax and enjoy a meal while trying to feed a babe at the same time.

The babe will fall into any routine you wish so long as you are consistent.

DO NOT ENCOURAGE the child to feed himself until he is much older. He has no sense of direction especially when handling a spoon!

§

73

WEANING THE HANDICAPPED CHILD

1. Do not commence weaning before six months.
2. Aim at cutting out milk if possible not later than two weeks after the commencement of weaning.
3. Make certain the child quenches his thirst with water during and between meals.
4. Possetting is a sure sign of too little water.
5. Do not be afraid of cutting out milk.

Again, as I say, it is difficult to advise for a handicapped child because, as you know, the Type and Degree of handicap varies with each child.

Commence weaning at six months of age and FOLLOW ALL THE INSTRUCTIONS CAREFULLY. Instead of using a household mincer use a food grinder for the first two to four weeks followed by a household mincer. The use of the food grinder, the feeding bottle for water · and the spoon handle for feeding may be required for an indefinite

97

period, depending on the handicap. DO NOT BE OVER ANXIOUS.
The child will progress in his own time.

What I am concerned about, and I hope you are, is the cutting out of
the milk! Cut it out about one or two weeks after the commencement of
weaning. Cereal foods and savoury which contain cereal upset the milk
balance which is so necessary before the age of six months. After that
age the handicapped child no longer requires the high fat and sugar content of milk. The one week time limit gives you some idea as to how
long the complete weaning may take. Of course under the circumstances
this period may vary. Aim for the one to two weeks and you will not go
far wrong.

I do not say, following instructions cures a handicap; no one can do
that! But it does mean a quieter contented child. Again, according to
the handicap. When relief Health Visiting I found so many parents
resigned to their UNNECESSARILY restless children. They were afraid
of my advice because they had not heard it before or they were afraid of
the results. Life was difficult enough without adding complications.
Should you have been in possession of this book from the beginning,
few, if any, complications would have arisen. Acquiring the book at a
later date some difficulties may arise. Somewhere, in the book, you will
find the answer.

FOODS TO AVOID DURING AND AFTER WEANING

1. Sugary drinks, squashes, fruit juices in any form.
2. Cereals in any form including rusks.
3. Potatoes.
4. Banana.
5. Tinned fruits.
6. Ice cream.
7. Yoghurt.
8. Custard.
9. MILK and MILKY DRINKS.
10. Sweets and chocolate.
11. Bread.
12. Cakes and biscuits.
13. Soups (except when home made and used as a gravy).
14. Tinned and convenience foods.
15. Milk puddings.
16. Pasta.
17. Sausages.
18. Rissoles.
19. Fish fingers.
20. Fish cakes.
21. Pastries.

Reading through these food items to be avoided it will gradually occur to you the foods I have mentioned are starchy sugary and bulky. Incapable of sustaining a child for five hours. The child slips into a two-hourly routine, causing all the problems of Wrong Feeding (Nos 49-58).

These foods are expensive when their sustaining power is compared to that of meat, fish, eggs and cheese. In fact these high protein foods are cheapest in the long run.

Full co-operation of relations and grand-parents is necessary. When these people are visited by young people ALL these foods appear, as if by magic, as a wonderful treat on the tea table.

Between the ages of two to three years the child may be invited to birthday parties. Do not spoil the party. Allow him to eat anything he wishes. The next day he will be quite happy to return to his own routine. PROVIDING the exception does not become the rule – in other words – too many parties!

§

75

PROTEIN FOODS FOR WEANING

1. Beef; casseroled or roasted. Mince after cooking.
2. Lamb; casseroled or roasted. Mince after cooking.
3. Chicken; casseroled or roasted. Mince after cooking.
4. Turkey; casseroled or roasted. Mince after cooking.
5. Rabbit; casseroled. Mince after cooking.
6. Duck; casseroled. Mince after cooking.
7. Pork; casseroled or roasted. Mince after cooking.
8. Corned beef; mash. Use later during weaning.
9. Spam mince. Use later during weaning.
10. Hare; casseroled. Mince after cooking.
11. Bacon; ALWAYS boil or roast. Mince after cooking.
12. Ham; ALWAYS boil or roast. Mince after cooking.
13. Liver; casseroled. Mash with a fork after cooking.
14. Kidney; casseroled. Mash with a fork after cooking.
15. Sweetbreads; casseroled. Mash with a fork after cooking.
16. Brains; casseroled. Mash with a fork after cooking.
17. Venison; casseroled or roasted. Mince after cooking.
18. Fish; Steamed or fried. Discard batter.
19. Cheese; ALWAYS shredded. UNCOOKED. do not use processed cheese.
20. Eggs; ALWAYS scrambled.
21. AVOID: pies, pastries, rissoles, fishcakes, sausages, fish fingers and, in the early days, butchers' mince.

I have endeavoured to compose a reasonable list of protein foods to use during early and later weaning and give adequate choice. These foods

100

may be given cold; especially at breakfast time, saving fussing around at 7.00 am.

In the supermarkets, chicken, rabbit and turkey are sold by the joint. At the beginning this is a suitable amount but later a larger quantity will be necessary.

Foods like bacon, ham, liver and cheese may be added to other foods for variety or when you have under-estimated Junior's appetite and the prepared food is running short. At least it will save you having to prepare other foods.

I have advised you to give butchers' mince during later weaning. Primarily because the quality varies so much. Secondly it depends just how good a cook you are, whether the end product is lumpy or not. I could never manage to cook butchers' mince without lumps, but that did not matter; I am an adult. As an alternative I suggest you purchase stewing or frying steak, cook it yourself and then mince it. To make it worthwhile you may cook a reasonable amount, prepare it and put half in the deep freeze. Again this prevents fiddling.

You may prefer to leave the venison, hare, duck and pork until weaning is established. On the other hand, should the family be having these foods there is no harm offering a small quantity to the child. If accepted you may continue.

ALL PROTEIN FOODS MUST BE MINCED OR GRATED UNTIL THE AGE OF TWO YEARS OLD WHEN THE CHILD HAS HIS FULL COMPLEMENT OF TEETH.

N.B. As a result of BSE offal is, at the time of writing, unobtainable. At a later date it may re-appear on the shelves.

No 76:

VARIATIONS OF PROTEINS FOR WEANING

1. Scrambled eggs.
2. Fish and cheese.
3. Fish and scrambled eggs.
4. Liver and finely grated cheese.
5. Liver and bacon.
6. Liver, bacon/ham and scrambled egg.
7. Grated cheese and casseroled beef.
8. Grated cheese and roast meat gravy.
9. Cheese and casseroled liver gravy.
10. Scrambled egg and grated cheese. Add the cheese after the egg is cooked.
11. Scrambled egg and tomatoes; tinned or fresh.
12. Rabbit and chicken.

How many times have I heard mothers saying "What on earth can I give them?" And that remark refers to older children who can eat anything. When there is a crisis I have heard this cry also, especially when the mother is tired or sickening for flu. "What do I give the baby – in the process of weaning?"

I decided to draw up a list of variations to give a few ideas, to save you having to think.

There are a few items you must ALWAYS have in your cupboard, freezer or fridge. (1) Tinned tomatoes. (2) grated cheese. (3) MINCED bacon or ham. (4) Eggs. From these foods you have six meals for the babe to last for two days, to give you time to sort yourself out. I shall spell them out for you because when you are tired or sick, thinking is the last thing you want to do. (1) Scrambled eggs and tomatoes. (2) Bacon/ham and egg. (3) Cheese and egg. (4) Cheese and tomato. (5) Cheese and bacon/ham. (6) Bacon/ham and tomato.

The tinned tomatoes may be given with any meal to replace vegetables. The repetition is not ideal but this food for two days will not hurt the babe but it will give you a chance to recover. In spite of the repetition the babe is not given the same flavour twice in succession. Anyone helping you will have no problems producing meals for the babe using these foods.

EGGS MUST ALWAYS BE GIVEN SCRAMBLED. Babes and young children dislike boiled or poached eggs intensely. They spit out the white which is the important part of the egg. Boiled eggs FEEL like LUMPY CUSTARD. the only way they are prepared to eat eggs is when they are scrambled.

Do not discard – waste – any scrambled egg left over from the meal. The reminder can be used in conjunction with another meal and even reheated in a small heatproof basin in a pan of water. So the mums tell me!

§

77

VEGETABLES FOR WEANING

1. Cabbage.
2. Cauliflower.
3. Spring Greens.
4. Brussel Sprouts.
5. Leeks.
6. Onions.
7. Beetroots.
8. Celery.
9. Tomatoes.
10. Parsnips.
11. Cucumbers.
12. Kale.
13. Aubergines.
14. Peppers; green, red and yellow.
15. Avocado pears.
16. Spinach.
17. Chicory.
18. Broccoli.
19. Fennel.
20. Carrots.
21. Turnips.
22. Swedes.

Apart from listing the usual vegetables I have included some of the more unusual ones in case you had doubts regarding their suitability.

Vegetables are a COMPLIMENT to protein NOT A SUBSTITUTE. They may be cooked in bulk to cover nine meals; they keep well in a cold fridge. You may find it more convenient to cope with vegetables along with family meals – so long as there are vegetables prepared in readiness for the child's meal when he requires it. They need not be reheated – which will over cook them but added to warm or cold food.

During the early day liquidising the vegetable is a good idea because of the tougher leaves and stalks which contain the flavour. (Do not add liquid)

Use the pips and skins of the tomatoes and cucumbers, liquidised. they are a good substitute for soups and gravies.

Go carefully with the quantity of vegetables at the beginning. In conjunction with the fruits they must only produce a soft stool. Some vegetables have more effect on the bowels than others. Frequent runny stools DO NOT mean an allergy! Just the fact you have given too much. Cut the quantities but do not cut them out.

§

78

FRUITS FOR WEANING

FRESH FRUITS

1. Red currants.
2. Black currants.
3. Brambles.
4. Cherries.
5. Plums.
6. Strawberries.
7. Raspberries.
8. Loganberries.
9. Greengages.
10. Melon.
11. Oranges.
12. Apples.

DRIED FRUITS

1.   Apricots.
2.   Peaches.
3.   Apples.
4.   Pears.
5.   Currants.
6.   Sultanas.
7.   Prunes.
8.   Figs.
9.   Dates – for sweetening.

I commence with dried fruits. They are so much easier to cope with than fresh fruit. There is so much variety and it does not "Go Off" providing it is kept in air tight containers or jars.

Currants and sultanas require reconstituting also; I mention this as they are so often eaten in their dried state.

The fresh fruit loses its bloom soon after purchase and deteriorates before the babe can eat it. The currants and berries make a pleasant change when in season and frozen for later use. Cook three different types of fruit to cover nine meals. At the beginning in small quantities: only VERY SMALL quantities to be given at one time. The larger fruits such as apples and oranges are best given when weaning is well established but ONLY 1/4 at one time.

The juice of fresh or dried fruits used with gelatine makes beautiful jellies for a sweet. It is a change of texture. Mixed juices may also be used. Avoid, if possible, giving the same flavour twice in succession.

Take care on how much you give at a time. Fruit is required three times a day, single flavours or mixed. Just enough to produce a regular soft formed stool. If the stool is relaxed the child has not an allergy. Cut down the quantity but still give three times a day.

DO NOT GIVE BANANAS OR TINNED FRUIT.

TRAVELLING WITH A YOUNG CHILD.

1. When artificially fed, make up sufficient number of feeds to extend over the travelling time. Have an extra feed to cater for a hold up, particularly if on a long journey.
2. Do not forget the drinks of water between feeds.
3. The bottles may not be authentic feeding bottles; any bottle that will hold a teat is adequate.
4. Have a sterile container to hold the sterile teats.
5. Have another container to hold the discarded teats,
6. For the child on solids place each meal into a separate container.
7. It will not hurt the child to have a series of cold meals. Carry an extra one in case of a delay en route.
8. COLD WATER IS ESSENTIAL FOR NURSING MOTHERS, also for the children.
9. Purchase an insulated bag to hold this equipment and two "Freeze Blocks" to keep the food fresh and cool.

An insulated bag and two or three "Freeze blocks" is ideal for carrying the equipment. Whatever the means of transport or the length of journey the insulated bag is really a necessity for your own relaxation and the babe's comfort.

The feeding bottles require corks or screw tops. Ordinary screw top plastic bottles are excellent and certainly cheaper. There are many different shapes and sizes to choose from but a teat must GRIP FIRMLY to them. Take a teat along with you when purchasing. After making your choice, try the teat.

The plastic containers are also required. The first for the sterile teats, the second for the discarded ones. When purchasing this equipment do not forget bottles for the drinks of water, plus the necessary teats.

Breast fed babies are more straight forward except they require bottles and teats containing water. A VERY ADEQUATE SUPPLY IS NECESSARY FOR THE NURSING MOTHER. THERE IS NOTHING LIKE TRAVELLING LONG DISTANCES TO REDUCE THE QUANTITY OF BREAST MILK. She becomes dehydrated and at the end of the journey she will have no milk. This is one reason why I STRONGLY recommend one breast – one feed. There is always 1/2 a feed in reserve.

When it comes to heating feeds or water place the bottle under the armpit. A feed will take approximately one hour to heat up. On a long journey or a day out there is no reason to stop the car – especially on a Bank Holiday!

A toddler or a baby-toddler will not object to a session of cold meals. After all, by the time they have fiddled about, the hot meal would be cold. Use one container for the protein and vegetables and another for the fruit. Each meal is to be catered for in this manner. A good idea is to have an extra prepared meal for use after arrival or for breakfast next morning should you arrive late at night or be held up en route.

A "Golf" umbrella is a must. It may be used as a windshield or protection from direct sunlight.

Once you have settled in after reaching your destination your host and hostess may wish to take you out for the day. Take this equipment with you. Failing to do so means "I think we had better stop at the next Motorway Service." Or "Will you stop when you can find a place!" This means you are probably in the centre of town where there is no parking!! The babe begins to cry and then yell. Everyone in the car is distressed. The same goes for a bus tour; there is nothing worse than having a crying child on board!

DO NOT have the babe or young child sitting on your knee. They get too hot absorbing the heat from your body. have the carrycot on your knee if you must and the older child strapped to the seat.

Providing you have been Clock Feeding (See No 46) you are aware of the time of the child's natural functions. This again saves fussing with the child. With a little practice a toddler or young child will be prepared to use the potty on the car floor or, in a bus, in a container on your knee with a screw topped lid.

During World War II the long distance trains were crowded to say the least, both in the compartments and corridors, with army, navy and RAF personnel travelling with full kit. The blackout was in force. All windows were closed and the atmosphere blue with cigarette and pipe tobacco smoke.

Christmas 1941 in such a train, a THREE WEEK old baby travelled in a wicker clothes basket, with a handle on each end, from Edinburgh to Reigate, change of stations and so on: a twenty hour journey. The mattress was clean nappies, a pillow case for the soiled ones, a bottle of oil and a sponge bag for the used oiled swabs.

The babe was bottle fed. In an attache case were packed brown sauce and ketchup bottles and similar, each containing the necessary feeds and drinks of water. No fancy feeding bottles in those days! A jar for sterile teats, a jar for used ones, a measuring jug and a bottle brush. The kit bag, the rifle and the attache case were laid and secured across the basket – with the baby in it, of course.

A space was made on the luggage rack for the basket and the babe. When feeding and drinks of water time came around every two hours, down came the basket on the passenger's knees. The bottles were warmed in the mother's or father's armpit. the armed forces were most impressed; they must tell their wives! During all that journey there was not one whimper from the babe.

How many of you modern mums could cope with that horrendous 20-hour journey without "Mod Cons"? This goes to prove what a contented clock-fed baby is capable of coping with.

§

80

THE HYPER-ACTIVE CHILD OR THE CHILD WHO WILL NOT SLEEP

1. Wrong feeding – too much starchy and sugary food.
2. Thirst – too many vitamin drinks, manufactured squashes or milky drinks such as tea.
3. Lack of routine due to wrong feeding.
4. Tinned and other prepared foods, convenience foods high cereal content for thickening etc.
5. Additives.
6. Lack of water.

The hyper-active babe or child IS THE ONE who will not sleep. This is no fantasy and is becoming a very popular subject for discussion groups and TV programmes. Various causes are given, the main one being the presence of additives in the food.

In spite of all the discussions, consultations and TV programmes no one has suggested the cause to be wrong feeding and thirst! By thirst I mean LACK OF WATER. NOT lack of FLUIDS, which are entirely different to water.

For a child under six months read about feeding (breast and bottle). Compare what you read with what you are doing. Usually the babe is thirsty. This is all contained in the articles on Feeding (Nos 33-48) and Cries of a Baby (Nos 22-32).

Now!! – just what food and drinks really contain these harmful additives? Really think! They are the prepared convenience foods and drinks; squashes etc. These convenience foods and drinks should never be included in the child's diet at all!!

Children who have these foods consume an abnormal amount of starches and sugars giving an excessive amount of energy. An abnormal amount of energy means without a doubt there is a lack of protein in the diet to cope with the wear and tear caused by hyper-activity.

These children have no feeding routine, as stated in the Child Who Will Not Eat (No 81). They are always on the want. The drinking of water is usually unknown to these children They drink vast quantities of these fancy drinks because these drinks ONLY TEMPORARILY quench their thirst.

The natural functions of the bowels and bladder may be badly affected. Constipation, diarrhoea and bed wetting, potty tantrums, and the soling of pants, not to mention cramp.

Over six months of age read the articles on Weaning (Nos 68-80) regardless of age. Feeding routine, also a list of foods available and the list of foods to avoid, are included in this article. Again compare what you are reading with what you are doing, which means what you are giving the child to eat or drink.

Once the correct food is given life will improve but be prepared for difficulties with water drinking. The child will strongly resist. DO NOT WEAKEN. No one can exist without water. ALWAYS have water available in a cup. Sooner or later the child MUST drink. After that drink of water there is no further problem. In the case of a resistant baby use a plastic bottle and a small-holed teat. Turn the baby's head slightly to the side and squeeze a small quantity of water at a time into the baby's CHEEK. This method ensures the water trickles down the throat without choking the babe. Again, once the water problem is solved all is quiet. As you will observe water is the ONLY fluid that really quenches thirst.

I now hear you ask "Why has the Additive Problem become so common?" Since World War II, we have become an affluent society with money in our pockets to purchase those expensive convenience foods and drinks. Competition...? Each firm endeavouring to make their goods the most attractive especially when similar goods manufactured by other firms are displayed on the same shelf!

Follow the comprehensive list of weaning foods. There is an ample variety – and bear in mind the list of foods to avoid.

Again a word of warning. – DO NOT RESORT TO SEDATIVES. You are storing up trouble for yourself and your child in later years. For example drug addiction, whether medical sedatives or "hard drugs."

Within a day or two the child/babe will settle. Somewhere in the feeding instructions from birth (depending on the age of the child) you will find the answer.

THE OLDER CHILD

81

THE CHILD WHO WILL NOT EAT

CAUSES: – THE CHILD IS NOT HUNGRY! — WHY NOT?

1. EARLY weaning
2. Milk and squash drinking etc.
3. Sweets, chocolates, ice-cream, yoghurt, biscuits etc.
4. "Always on the want" for something to eat or drink.
5. Lumpy – Soppy foods (some of the tinned/jar variety).
6. Too much choice.
7. Lack of variety.
8. Badly prepared food.
9. Illness or the onset of illness.
10. Teething.

CURE:

1. DO NOT UNDERESTIMATE YOUR CHILD'S WILL-POWER! IT INCREASES WITH AGE!
2. DO NOT COAX under any circumstances.
3. USE ONLY the listed foods mentioned in the articles on Weaning (Nos 68-80).
4. MAKE THE CHILD HUNGRY AND KEEP HIM HUNGRY by offering a VERY small portion of food for his breakfast. If not eaten in $1/2$ hour, remove it.
5. NO food or drink of ANY kind to be given between meals (5 hours), ONLY water.
6. KEEP HIM HUNGRY BY OFFERING ANOTHER SMALL MEAL at lunch time. If eaten, refuse a second helping.
7. NO ALTERNATIVE OFFERED IF A MEAL IS REFUSED.
8. Offer WATER EVERY HOUR until the child is eating normally, then during meals and in between.

9.   Arrange meals 7.00 am, midday, and 5.00 pm. The last meal in the evening may be over five hours after the previous meal but NEVER under. A second helping may be given if necessary.

10. BE FIRM when dealing with food. Act as if you are uncon-cerned whether he eats his food or starves for the want of it.

11. DO NOT ARGUE OR THREATEN.

12. By 5.00 pm (6.00 or 7.00 pm on the first day only) the last meal of the day will be eaten and enjoyed. Once a solid meal has been eaten your problems are over!!

13. Continue from now on giving as much solid food (Protein) as the child can eat and water to drink.

14. When sick (ill) ALWAYS give water to drink before and after anything to eat or drink.

15. REFER TO THE ARTICLES ON WEANING (Nos 68-80) AND MILK (Nos 28-45), NO MATTER WHAT THE AGE OF THE CHILD. Contained in these articles is all the information regarding routine etc. for a child of any age.

"My child will not eat The doctor tells me there is nothing wrong. So long as he drinks milk he will come to no harm! I am so worried. He has not eaten anything for days: I cook but the food is wasted!"

How often I have listened to this cry for help from tired, anxious parents who have reached the point of desperation!

These children are so restless. They niggle all day! First they want to be outside, then they want to be in! They will not settle. In other words they must always be amused. This behaviour is not only confined to their own home, but wherever they go. Because of interruptions no conversation takes place between mother and friend. Eventually she gives up, wishing she had not gone visiting. A disruptive child is better in one's own home than in someone else's.

The PRIMARY cause of this problem is early weaning (cereals and milk drinking). The upsetting of the milk intake before 6 months. The SECOND PRIMARY cause is sickness (illness). These early weaners are usually subject to bronchitis due to excessive weight gain. So much milk and sugary drinks are given during illness the child is prevented from gaining his normal appetite.

The first sign of trouble is when the child develops strong likes and dislikes and soon needs coaxing to eat. A feast and famine technique; consuming a large meal of food he likes and starving until something else he likes appears on the menu, usually ice-cream or similar. WASTE

NO MORE TIME! From time immemorial food was and is meant to be enjoyed. A faddy child is deprived of this enjoyment.

Up to the age of 2 years the child is little of a problem. Eight hours without food after mid-day with only water to drink sorts things out. he is fractious, of course, during this period but do not be concerned. It only lasts until the waiting period is over. It is a good idea to offer a child of any age food he has refused in the past. He is sure to refuse it. This method brings about more rapid results.

The two to five year olds present a more difficult problem but still offer foods they dislike until they come to terms.

The problem often arises because you are tired and also because of your child's will power. DO NOT UNDER ESTIMATE THIS WILL POWER!! Some of these children can refuse food and water for THREE DAYS!!

One mother told me she could happily throw her four year old out of the window she was so exasperated. When I met "Young Madam" I could see just why and could sympathise with the poor mother had she done just that! I advised the parents what to do and they decided to be co-operative. The tantrums were terrible! After all; these sorts of children have NEVER been thwarted in their young lives.

I spent time daily with the parents to give them moral support and encouragement. On the third day "Madam" had still refused food and drink. Suddenly she realised I was responsible for her predicament. A tantrum was thrown for my benefit. It lasted non-stop for 2 HOURS. Tired out she fell asleep for four hours. On awakening she went to the tap and helped herself to a long drink of water. Afterwards, at 5.00 pm, she ate a good meal, AND ENJOYED IT! In all probability it was the first meal she had ever really enjoyed in spite of the fact it was food she had disliked in the past! From then on the child became happy and contented.

This is an exaggerated instance but it demonstrates to parents as to how long they must be prepared to resist a toddler. The answer is INDEFINITELY! YOU WILL WIN IN THE END – YOU CANNOT FAIL!!! You place the child in the position of VOLUNTARY COMPULSION!

I was called to another child; a boy of 6 1/2 years old. Since birth he had not had a complete nights sleep. (Neither had his parents). He would refuse to go to bed. He woke up several times during the night SCREAMING with pains in his legs. Repeated visits to the GP plus sedatives – no results. Repeated visits to the Paediatrician – no joy there. He was referred to the Psychiatrist – THE DIAGNOSIS? — WAIT FOR IT!!! It is all in his mind. He is demanding attention! That poor little boy, I could have wept for him. He had pains in his legs without a doubt!..HE HAD CRAMP!!!

Being 6 1/2 years old I discussed the problem with him. His parents were at the end of their tether. He was deprived of food all day. He was more disruptive than usual. At about 8.00 pm he ate a very satisfying meal (with a second helping) – and ASKED to go to bed and had the first full night's sleep since birth. Within three days, as I promised him, drinking plenty of water and eating correct food there would be no more cramp.

These two instances are exceptional but it does illustrate how children and parents can suffer because of wrong feeding.

The boy who suffered cramp later told his mother his concentration had improved and he could get his lessons finished before anyone else in the class. A five year old who had some distance to walk to school told his mother he did not get tired running to school and could now keep up with his big brother. Both ex-sufferers asked their parents to continue with their "New Food". I have had similar results reported to me by parents of children whose bad eating habits I have corrected.

BED WETTING

CAUSES: For the older child

1.   Lack of protein.
2.   Too much starchy food.
3.   Too much sugary food.
4.   All juices, squashes, pop etc.
5.   Lack of water.
6.   Too much pocket money to purchase rubbishy foods etc.

CURE:

1.   THREE "Dinners" a day consisting of meat, fish, eggs or cheese plus vegetables and a SMALL helping of potato, followed by fruit and an OCCASIONAL banana.
2.   Refer to article Protein Foods for the Older Child (No 84).
3.   Give JUST sufficient fruit and vegetables to produce a normal soft stool.
4.   Refer to article Foods to Avoid (74 & 84) for the Older Child.
5.   Nothing between meals except WATER to drink.
6.   At least five hours between meals.
7.   Do not give the same flavours of foods twice in one day.

A very distressing and anti-social complaint, embarrassing to both parents and child and, what is so appalling, this can continue nightly until the teens or even later.

The usual attempt at a cure is the restriction of fluids from approximately 2.00 pm – to no avail. The next step is the use of the bell attached to a wired sheet. When the child just begins to wet the bed the bell goes off like a fire alarm, waking the child, the remainder of the household and possibly the neighbours, depending on the thickness of the wall. Even this does not always cure the complaint. The final useless advice is – ignore it – the child will grow out of the habit. The dis- . tressed parents and child are left.

These children do not have a high protein diet. They eat the sweet and sugary foods listed in Foods to Avoid During and After Weaning (No 74). These starchy, sugary foods make the individual very thirsty. To overcome their thirst, quantities of pop, squashes and juices are drunk. These drinks in themselves have a high sugar content. They ONLY APPEAR TO QUENCH THE CHILD'S THIRST. By the time the sugar and starches in the food and drinks have been digested all the fluid is ready to be discharged (at an alarming rate) as urine during the night. Strong urine it is too!

After all that I return to the old chestnut – WRONG FEEDING!!!

Refer to Protein Foods for the Older Child (No 84). I may appear stupid referring to foods when the child is 10 years old! These are foods children of all ages must have and also refer to Foods to Avoid for the Older Child (No 84), again regardless of age. Foods to Avoid; you may think of others but at least I have given you a start.

Children who attend Day Nurseries or Play Groups are usually given a drink during the morning or the afternoon. Please request that your child only has water. If the child is at the centre for lunch, provide YOUR OWN high protein meal plus dried fruit for your child. It may prove difficult for a school child to return home for lunch. Send his lunch to school with him, using plastic cutlery and crockery in case of loss.

As time progresses and you persevere less urine will be passed at a time until the bladder can give sufficient warning to disturb the child and give him time to reach the toilet.

Do not restrict the amount of water the child requires but ONLY GIVE WATER TO DRINK. No child drinks more water than he requires.

Do not despair! I cured a 15 year old boy in four weeks so that he could go camping with the Scouts. There is a cure – DEPENDING ON CORRECT FOOD AND DRINK (see Article No. 84).

SOILED PANTS

CAUSES: For the Older Child.

1. Lack of protein.
2. Too much starchy food.
3. Too much sugary food.
4. All squashes, pop etc.
5. Lack of water.
6. Too much pocket money to purchase rubbishy foods etc.

CURE:

1. THREE dinners a day consisting of meat, fish, eggs or cheese, plus vegetables and a small helping of potato followed by fruit and an occasional banana.
2. Refer to article Protein foods for the Older Child (No 84).
3. Just sufficient fruit and vegetables to produce a normal soft stool.
4. Refer to article Foods to Avoid for the Older Child (No 84).
5. NOTHING between meals except WATER to drink.
6. At least five hours between meals.
7. Do not give the same flavour twice in one day.

This article really deals with the school child as the pre-school children's problem is coped with in the articles on weaning. Many parents are under the impression that once a child has reached the age of two years they are at liberty to eat anything they wish. Often they do so with dire results.

Heading the list of causes I again return to the old chestnut, LACK OF PROTEIN. I repeat: PROTEIN is the MOST SUSTAINING FOOD there is. Therefore the CHEAPEST in comparison to the quantity of other foods required.

These starchy sugary foods are bulky and expensive. They form a . vicious circle. The child is always picking at biscuits, ice-cream, sweets and so on. These foods make the child thirsty. They are not water drinkers – instead they drink quantities of sugary drinks – squashes, pop, juices etc. These sugary drinks only TEMPORARILY quench thirst - hence the quantities consumed. ALL this excessive sugar, including sweets, acts as an irritant to the bowels causing the uncontrollable relaxed stools.

The child's co-operation is vital. He must be guided by the parents decision if in doubt. As a school child his temptations are many. Any diversion prolongs the problem. You must show patience and encouragement.

It must be three "dinners" a day. Cut out the fruit and vegetables except for a small potato until the bowels become less frequent. Then introduce VERY GRADUALLY the vegetables and fruits.

There must be at least five hours between meals with only water to drink. Do not ration the protein. He has a great deal of lee-way to make up after consuming all this sugar and starch.

I have compiled a list of Proteins for the Older Child, also Foods to Avoid for the Older Child (both No 84), which I hope will be of help to you. You may be able to add to both lists.

During the school holidays is the best time to cure this problem. Once cured the child may enjoy birthday parties and so on as they come with no ill effects. Afterwards they are happy to return to their three meals a day.

A four year old boy never wet his pants but always soiled them. All the fancy excuses were made; he is looking for attention, cuddle him more often, give him a reward when he uses his pot. I suggested to the mother that sometime in the past he must have been constipated. She doubted this but agreed to follow my advice. He was given Protein for Toddlers (No 84). After a number of weeks he sat on his pot and used it. he said "It didn't hurt Mummy".

As a matter of interest this was the mother of the babe who ate the 1/2 lb steak on a cold day after sitting outside in his pram.

On the other end of the scale, when in school I saw an eight year old boy walking down the corridor with a teacher holding his hand. He was sobbing his heart out. He had soiled his pants; it was all down his legs in his socks and shoes. The GP was tired of the mother haunting the surgery. He passed her and the child on to me – fortunately. Being eight years old and there being other children in the house he was capable of helping himself to sweets, biscuits, pop and so on. He soiled the living room carpet, the bathroom carpet; unable to get his pants down in time. Even the stairs up to the flat were soiled.

It was the beginning of the summer holidays. I visited daily. It took a couple of weeks to convince the boy I was trying to help him and how necessary it was to ask his mother what he could eat and what not. After co-operating it suddenly struck him that he could reach the bathroom and the loo without disaster. He returned to school a confident child. DOES THAT GIVE YOU CONFIDENCE? Do not give up hope. AGAIN; CORRECT FOOD IS THE ANSWER.

During this period Grandparents visited, always bringing sweets in spite of the mother's pleas. On my advice all soiled clothing would be put into a carrier bag and hung on the Grandparents' front door handle! They got the message and brought meat, eggs and fish instead. Sometimes drastic measures are called for.

§

84

PROTEIN FOODS FOR THE OLDER CHILD

1. Beef.
2. Lamb.
3. Chicken.
4. Turkey.
5. Rabbit.
6. Duck.
7. Pork.
8. Corned Beef.
9. Spam.
10. Hare.
11. Bacon.
12. Ham.
13. Liver.
14. Kidney.
15. Cooked meats from the counter.
16. Game Birds.
17. Venison.
18. Fish.
19. Cheese.
20. Eggs.

These foods may be cooked in a variety of ways.

You will probably observe they are almost exactly the same foods listed for weaning. The only difference is there is no limit as to the way they are cooked. these foods are a MUST before and during exams to produce sound sleep and concentration.

FOODS TO AVOID FOR THE OLDER CHILD

1. Sugary drinks and squashes, pop etc. in any form.
2. Cereals in any form.
3. Tinned fruit.
4. Ice-cream
5. Yoghurt.
6. Custard.
7. Milk and milky drinks.
8. Sweets and chocolate.
9. Bread.
10. Cake and biscuits.
11. Tinned and convenience foods.
12. Milk Puddings.
13. AN EXCESSIVE amount of pies, pasta, sausages, rissoles, fish-cakes and fish fingers.

These foods, because of their sugary and starchy contents, are capable of causing disturbed rest. Avoid these foods especially during exam periods. The exception to the rule is when the child is invited to birthday parties or at Christmas.

85

POCKET MONEY AND OTHER INCOME.

1. Pocket money must be enough but no more.
2. Permanent savings, (Saving Certificates etc.) must amount to 1/5 of the total income.
3. Board and lodging must amount to 1/5 of the total income.
4. Spending money; the remaining 2/5 of the total income.
5. Paper rounds, car washing etc. the same rules apply, viz. 3/5 to be handed over to the parents.
6. Gifts of money (Christmas, birthday), 1/2 for permanent saving 1/2 for spending.
7. With payment of wages or unemployment benefit POCKET MONEY CEASES!! BUT 3/5 still to be handed over.
8. DO NOT WEAKEN TO PLEADINGS for loans, reduction in Board & Lodging or for extra money. The youngster must learn the hard way and home is the best place to learn. It is a hard lesson.

Avoid the mistake of handing the child ONLY HIS SPENDING MONEY WITH THE STATEMENT "I have kept 2/5 for your Board & Lodging and 1/5 for savings" Hand over the TOTAL amount and wait until the 3/5 are returned to you. This has a psychological effect. Handing back money is not pleasant! Do not feel guilty; this pocket money, no matter how little, had to be worked for and tax paid on it – by the parents.

I can hear some of you say "I have four children; I can't afford all that money per week". Alright. No one said you had to. The pocket money is paid in accordance with your financial circumstances, PLUS the whole of the Board and Lodging money. 3/5 of the total is handed back. The Board and Lodging money is returned to the household purse. The 1/5 is used for Saving Certificates.

I do urge parents to try their utmost to save this Board and Lodging money; if not all at least some, no matter how small, towards the child's future. KEEP the child in ignorance of your saving his Board and Lodging otherwise he will get the idea you are playing games and the money he hands over to you is his by right! Well – It isn't!

Make certain he understands the 1/5 of his income is for the purchase of Saving Certificates.

Some parents will object to the "Off-takes" but consider...! Their friends expect to be fed, and wear and tear of the carpet, chairs and so on can be excessive, depending on the size of the family. Should there be wastage of food and unwarranted abuse of the home, increase the Board and lodging from 2/5 to 3/5 of the income (leaving 1/5 for spending money). You will be amazed at the results!!!

Strange as it may seem it is the parents who have the least money to spare for replacements in the home who have children, also wage-earners, with no consideration for the home and objecting to paying their way or taking an active part in the upkeep.

It is these children and teenagers with too much money and too much spare time who are the ones to roam the streets in gangs, getting into mischief with glue-sniffing, drugs, and so on. WHY...? Because of the excessive wear and tear in the home and the frustration of the misguided parents the home ceases to be attractive and comfortable.

In the affluent homes this Board and Lodging money may not be required for housekeeping. The less affluent families may require a portion of it. Others may need all of the Board and Lodging money.

There is no need to supervise the 2/5 spending money. Offer advice by all means, especially regarding SAVING for hobby equipment, holidays etc. Especially the latter; if no holiday spending money is saved - TOO BAD! DO NOT WEAKEN AND DO NOT ARGUE. Junior may be miserable; no spending money for holidays! but he has learnt a very important lesson; MONEY CAN ONLY BE SPENT ONCE!! This incident will not happen again.

DO NOT and I repeat DO NOT make excuses to give the child extra pocket money – by running messages, washing dishes and so on. These jobs are all part and parcel of belonging to a home and a community. This can change a generous caring child into a mercenary little so-and-so! You may disagree but keep your eyes and ears open! The majority of the elderly and handicapped who have jobs regularly done for them against those who are left, pay the young for their services. Grand parents are usually the victims of this practice. You, as parents, discuss your saving plans with these people and reason with them. Their co-operation is so important. Should they insist on payment, it should not amount to more than a few pence. Request this remuneration be handed over to you. This in turn, unbeknown to the child, is put into "Your" permanent savings for him.

As the child grows older, paper rounds, car washing, gardening, etc. are more time consuming and payment is acceptable. Again the rule applies: 3/5 handed over to the parents and 2/5 for free spending. EARNED INCOME INCREASES RESPONSIBILITIES – ANOTHER LESSON LEARNT!

As a teenager he may be unfortunate enough to go on the dole. Even so, ALL POCKET MONEY CEASES. This is a dangerous period both for parents and youngsters, the parents can so often become over-sympathetic. To the youngsters even the dole will appear so much after the restricted pocket money. INSIST that 3/5 is handed over. This also applies to wages. I hope at this stage the lesson of thrift and responsibility has been learnt by the young. The paying-up should not prove too difficult. I agree this does not leave all that amount of spare money, but it does encourage the youngster to spend discreetly and gives the incentive to find work – ANY KIND – working on his own or otherwise. There is such a thing as "Can't and Won't". They have the same results. In fact it makes the looking for work a voluntary compulsion!!

The paying-up at this stage again may not prove too difficult. Of course, inevitably, there will be the comment "You take nearly all my money; my friends are allowed to keep theirs". YOUR REPLY IS: "You pay your way at home or you keep your money to use for yourself in digs or a bed sit. AND you do NOT return once a week to eat us out of house and home AND expect to have your washing and ironing done. I give you two days to think it over before giving an answer". Under this pressure Junior will comply, life returns to normal and peace reigns once more. YOU NEVER ARGUE!!

No one can blame the teenagers. Trying it on is only natural. But it is you – parents – who determine the winner.

At this age the teenagers have become used to budgeting and thinking over plans before spending. This is a wonderful deterrent against buying way-out clothes and may also prove a strong barrier against drug addiction and, I may add, these very early marriages.

Reading through these pages you will notice that responsibility and permanent saving is the main theme. At the same time it may not have occurred to you these savings are the foundations towards a deposit for their own home. The habit is formed to save for this end. When the now young man or woman is seriously talking about saving for a home, imagine their joy and gratitude when presented with part of all the savings from their Board and Lodgings plus the 1/5 of their permanent savings. There is no need to say more.

Bear in mind all necessities for life are provided by the parents until the child is in receipt of wages or salary, so if the child runs short of money it is not the be all and end all of existence. Advise but do not nag. AND DO NOT WEAKEN. After all, the $^2/_5$ pocket money is theirs to save or spend and the LESSON MUST BE LEARNT THE HARD WAY!!

§

86

DANGER

1. There is always danger in life. It is the PARENTS' RESPONSIBILITY to protect the child.
2. When the babe FIRST attempts to climb the stairs, IMMEDI-ATELY CARRY THE CHILD TO THE TOP OF THE STAIRS AND TEACH HIM TO COME DOWN.
3. Repeat this operation until the babe is CAPABLE of coming down UNASSISTED.
4. This will take time and patience.
5. When the child is capable of descending unassisted there is no problem in climbing up.
6. I ALWAYS advise to keep the child under control when you are otherwise engaged. (Tether them or use a play pen.)
7. Do not always SEND your child out to play. TAKE him out, especially in a strange locality, and observe any dangers for yourself.
8. Draw attention to a particular danger as it arises.
9. Give precise instructions when the risk of danger is encoun-tered.
10. REPEAT the instructions EACH TIME also the reasons and consequences.
11. Make certain the child understands the instructions and, if old enough, repeats them.
12. The subjects cover the home, outside play, poisonous plants etc.
13. When you have gained your knowledge and thought about it, APPLY your knowledge and convey it in a simple manner in

accordance to the child's age and understanding. In other words; ask the youngster to suggest any other dangers.

14. PARENTS, DO YOUR HOMEWORK AND THINK!
15. You may miss your favourite programme – that is better than losing your child!

At the first sign of the babe (eight months onwards) becoming interested in stairs CARRY him to the TOP and TEACH him to come down, guiding his legs. Repeat this operation once or twice a day according to his age. (ALWAYS carry him to the TOP and help him to get used to heights). Continue this operation until you are certain he has mastered the art. AFTER THIS – stairs may be climbed on his own at leisure.

BEFORE the crawling stage the babe, when on the floor, would probably be on his tummy. One minute he was there, then suddenly he wasn't – you understand what I mean! This is your cue for restraining the child when you are occupied; cooking, washing, ironing, using the vacuum cleaner or whatever.

A playpen usually takes up too much room and is not capable of being placed where mother and child can maintain contact. Often they dislike playpens. The answer is restrain him. Use a good set of reins. Add sufficient length of clothes line to allow free movement to exclude the point of access to cooking stove, favourite ornaments, electric plugs and so on. Then attach the line to a door knob or a purpose-placed hook. The babe will not appreciate the restraint because of the free movement.

This method is most useful living in an upstairs flat while negotiating the pram or pushchair up or down stairs. This method of restraint cannot be over-emphasised. It can be used up to the age of 4 $1/2$ - 5 years, especially if the child is handicapped.

An unrestrained two year old was drowned in a fish pond. The mother was out shopping, the father was watching the cup final! In one of the North East mining villages the houses are built with long back yards with a door at the end leading out into the lane. A child of four years old was restrained with a line fixed to the kitchen door and long enough to give her the full length of the yard. The mother was upstairs working when she happened to look out of the window. Someone had been in and left the door wide open. The child was at the open lane door. A lorry passed and suddenly $1/2$ ton of loose coal was deposited at the door. Need I say more? Because the mother had taken my advice and tethered the child all was well. A pity the two year old was not tethered - she would not have been drowned.

125

Should danger be completely eliminated from the older childrens' lives they will create their own. For example adventure playgrounds. To a certain extent they are controlled. Outside the playground uncontrolled danger exists; railway embankments etc. As parents it is YOUR DUTY to supervise and educate your child. AND your responsibility if you fail to do so. There is no one else to blame.

So many parents have the habit of SENDING their children out to play without even asking where they intend to go or with whom. This is when glue sniffing and other evils rear their ugly heads. I beg of you to take your children FAIRLY REGULARLY out to play or for a walk, ESPECIALLY in a strange neighbourhood, to observe existing dangers for yourselves.

In the Winter you may teach your child to make a slide on the garden path. Great fun! Does it stop there? NO. Quite a difference to sliding on a pond covered with ice and hoare frost or in the main thoroughfare. The garden path is harmless – the pond and thoroughfare DANGEROUS. Did you explain the difference to your child? Were you aware there was a pond within reach of your home?.

How many of you pointed out a laburnum tree and its pods? wild mushrooms, toadstools, deadly nightshade, hemlock and others, and explained the danger in no uncertain terms? Do you recognise these things yourselves? If not I suggest you ask questions and learn, QUICK!

Another dangerous situation is falling into a river especially when in spate. This also includes a frozen pond. The instructions are DO NOT ATTEMPT to get your companion out – you can't – RUN LIKE THE WIND AND SHOUT LIKE MAD until someone more able than yourself will hear you and come to your aid. This could mean life or death. These instructions have proved effective in the past.

Workshop tools – there is no harm in tools, BE THEY hammers, chisels, lathes or whatever, PROVIDING THEY ARE USED CORRECTLY. When your boy or girl, no matter how young, is interested in your workshop give encouragement UNDER SUPERVISION. Allow the child to observe you working, describe the tool you require, its proper use and where to find it. Instruct him how to pick it up and pass it to you in the correct manner and then to accept it from you also in the correct manner. When finished demonstrate how to lay the tool down on the workbench instead of throwing it down. The youngster will learn quickly to recognise the name and for what purpose the tool is used.

The time comes when he wishes to use the tools himself. Providing you are satisfied as to his ability, ALLOW him to do so under your

STRICT SUPERVISION, using his own materials. Answer any questions and correct any mis-use. This is followed by the crunch; threaten in no uncertain terms, severe punishment should he ever abuse the tools. ABUSE SPELLS DANGER. After all, these tools are yours, they are valuable! You expect to find a sharp chisel when you return, not one chewed to bits after being used as a screw driver by Junior.

You may say it is easier to keep the workshop locked. Go ahead, lock it! What does that do? PRECISELY NOTHING!! One day the workshop could be left open by mistake. Then what? A very negative approach. And the result? Accidents. FORBID THE CHILD TO USE POWER TOOLS unless you are there. DISCONNECT THEM. IF POSSIBLE IMMOBILISE THE SOCKETS BY A MASTER FUSE OUT OF THE CHILD'S REACH. DO SO.

Many of you have no idea how involved you can become in your childrens' lives. It requires reading, asking questions and holding discussions until you get the correct answer. In other words – do your homework. The reward is great – a deep bond will be formed. You may miss your favourite programme. Rather than losing your child not only by death or accident but by the other various ways a child can be lost causing heart break!

§

87

FIGHTING

1. It is a natural thing to do.
2. Do not prevent it under any circumstances.
3. Aggravation.
4. The wrong one is usually blamed (the elder).
5. Jealousy.
6. Greed.
7. Telling tales.

The elder child has spent a number of years on his own and has had the privilege of having the full attention of his parents. Whatever he made with his constructive toys they were found the way he left them.

The Junior arrives on the scene. Approximately one year later life suddenly becomes disrupted! Time is spent constructing some play material and left while at school; along comes Junior and with one sweep of the hand he has scattered everything all over the place. Naturally the elder is annoyed and may chastise Junior. There is a loud yell followed by crying. The mother rushes into the room and immediately punishes the elder for hitting the young one. She had not seen what has happened. Many times it does not occur to her that Junior deserved what he got. There are lessons to be learnt.

The real trouble is where there is jealousy. This and greed go hand in hand. A much more difficult problem. It MUST be understood it is NOT the child's fault that he is jealous! It is yours! If in doubt read the article Immediately After the Baby is Born – The Toddler (No 20). Depending on the age of the older child depends how to treat the jealousy. The younger has one of life's lessons to learn here. Not to resist when the elder grabs his toys. The novelty will soon wear off when there is no resistance. Should you actually be on the spot when the grabbing occurs then, by all means deal with the situation in the appropriate manner. There is correction here without injustice.

Providing there is a good relationship from birth DO NOT INTERFERE. No harm has been done. As the children advance in age the fighting becomes noisier. Under these circumstances the roof is capable of coming off the house. Tell them to get outside, or if it is raining, into the next room. As if by magic the fighting stops. Taking up new positions to continue the fight where they left off is just not on! This applies even with their friends. They all retire to lick their wounds.

Amongst all this there could be tale telling. It is just a case of childish play: "He has hit me hard" one can ignore it. The answer is simple! Do not aggravate! Full Stop! With older children when life becomes more complicated, tale-telling cannot be ignored completely. For instance if one of the children is stealing money from the housekeeping purse or school, both children should be approached together and the problem is sorted out.

Because you have been wise parents regarding fighting and tale-telling you will observe as the children become adults they bear no resentment towards each other. They have their differences, of course, don't we all! The terrible malice is absent. The malice that is capable of breaking up families. Those unfortunate families are the ones, more often than not, who were not allowed to fight as children. Their differences were always settled for them by adults...fairly or otherwise as the case may be.

TELLING LIES

REASONS FOR LYING.

1. To play one parent against another for various reasons.
2. To avoid punishment.
3. Spite: revenge as a rule.
4. Compulsive lying: bullying.
5. Cheating (copying the work of others and presenting it as one's own).
6. Prestige: talking big.
7. Stealing: begins from the housekeeping purse.
8. White lies.

A child of 3¹/2 years is capable of lying. It is usual when one parent refuses a request and the other grants it. The question arises "What did your mother say?" Quick as a flash: "She said yes but I had to ask you!" BEWARE of this and note the words "She said yes...but". REFRAIN from answering. The two parents, when they compare notes, discover the child has lied. The child is confronted by both parents and the request refused for the obvious reason – lying.

At a young age children realise a lie can save them from punishment. Parents must always be on the alert for lying. NEVER THINK your child at any age, is amusing when he lies and therefore above average intelligence. FAR FROM IT! It is YOU who are failing in your duties as parents.

A young child may, for example, have deliberately vandalised a toy and then lied about it. There may have been previous warnings. Usually a slap on the hand is sufficient. Then make it clear to the child the second slap is for telling the lie. All that is required is a definite slap; not a hard one.

Numbers 4, 5, 6, 7 and 8 are connected with the older child. the seven year old and upward may not, necessarily be more calculating but the misdemeanour is of a more serious nature calling for sterner punishment. Always deprive the child of an appropriate privilege for the action and another for the lie. This also refers to corporal punishment.

A child of seven years, may, unfortunately, catch you out in a white lie and call you to task. I hope not in front of the person concerned! But if so, and if possible restrain with hand pressure or change of subject. Later there must be a question and answer session and a wee chat about not interrupting adults' conversation, making sure the child understands. It is important to explain only adults are allowed this privilege and when they are grown up they will fully understand why this is.

§

89

BULLYING.

1. Bullies act either on their own or in gangs.
2. The victim is ALWAYS smaller or weaker than themselves.
3. Bullying can commence AT ANY AGE in the home or elsewhere including school.
4. They are PERSISTENT liars.
5. The reason for bullying is often extortion; anything from toys to money, bicycles etc.
6. Jealousy; eg The feelings of an older child against a "Supposedly" spoilt younger one.
7. A younger child can bully an older child by spiteful acts.

Cases of bullying have increased by astronomical proportions. At first it could be dealt with by a reprimand in front of the whole school. A second demands CORPORAL PUNISHMENT, also in front of the whole school. UNFORTUNATELY corporal punishment is now banned from schools – more's the pity! It is the dread of the bullies to be caught, humiliated and punished in front of others, especially their victims. Possibly the bully can be placed in school where the maximum number of his peers can see him. Put him on a box away from the wall. His misdemeanours should be made clear; a notice at his feet proclaiming "I AM A BULLY". The old fashioned stocks would prove a certain cure! Public humiliation is correct punishment for a bully who has delighted in the public humiliation of others!

No parent need stand up and say "My child is not a bully". If they had been found out THEY JOLLY WELL ARE! This time he was caught, the other instances have passed un-noticed or unchecked by those in charge. If these parents had been at home instead of out, (as they usually), working for cigarette and holiday money and so they would have been around to have nipped the problem in the bud before it became really serious. I do admit working parents are at a disadvantage, but do not allow bullying to go unchecked.

Teachers have their hands tied, (and bullies know this), they are not allowed to touch these children, WHY? Because of the Local authorities, Parliament and other Organisations. What can the teachers do? Turn their heads the other way and disbelieve the bullied child?

Parents MUST DEMAND ACTION when attending Parent/Teacher meetings. Teachers, on the other hand, MUST DEMAND of the "Powers That Be" authority to act. Should the "Powers That Be" fail to comply I draw their attention to the facts:

THEY ARE MORE THAN INDIRECTLY RESPONSIBLE FOR:
1. Con Men.
2. Rapes – this is a very serious form of bullying.
3. Wife Bashing – again bullying.
4. Beating up victims to leave them lying injured.
5. Tying up and injuring the invalid and the elderly.
6. VERY IMPORTANT: – Child abuse.

It is not easy to be popular and at the same time do one's duty!

No 90:

DISCIPLINE

HOW TO ADMINISTER DISCIPLINE.

1. SAY what you mean.
2. MEAN what you say.
3. DO NOT IGNORE STONY SILENCE or NO for an answer.
4. MAKE SURE you are obeyed.
5. ASK with a "Please" and a "Thank you" regardless of age.
6. ORDER – again with a please and a thank you.
7. THREATEN – DO NOT LOSE YOUR TEMPER.
8. ACT – according to age and misdemeanour.

A contented toddler can easily be distracted from what he is doing. memories are short at this tender age. As they grow older self-will develops and increases with age. This is only natural. There would be some mental handicap present if this did not happen. A child under seven years of age is considered not fully capable of reason. Of course reason does not appear overnight, so one must presume it develops gradually. At five years of age, or under, Junior is quite capable of understanding the tone of voice and is capable of defying you.

While you are peeling potatoes you find the toddler scribbling on the wall. You yell "Stop that!" and you proceed to peel potatoes. Later you find Junior with a pair of scissors cutting up you cushions!! I can imagine what can happen after that! YOU LASH OUT! BEFORE you start on the toddler THINK! You said "Stop that". The toddler did obey you and did stop that – didn't he? What you omitted to say, (for example) was "Sit down beside me and tell me a story." Had you suggested that instead of yelling "Stop that!" no cushion would have been chopped up.

YOU ARE AT FAULT.

The action you take depends on the age and the misdemeanour. At first children may be deprived of goodies or privilege with satisfactory results.

Failing this corporal punishment is called for. BUT ONLY WHEN ALL ELSE FAILS.

HOW TO ADMINISTER CORPORAL PUNISHMENT.

1. ALWAYS BE IN FULL CONTROL OF THE CHILD.
2. FOLLOW the instructions and there is no chance of injuring the child and being guilty of battering.
3. THERE IS NO CHANCE of you losing your temper. The ASK, ORDER, THREATEN, ACT advice gives you the time to control yourself completely.
4. Take the child sideways to you. Place his legs between your knees and cross your ankles. This prevents the child from kicking or running away.
5. Bend him over, the arm next to you is kept straight ALONGSIDE your body and his.
6. His outside arm is held by you lightly by the wrist above his head.
7. His head is under your arm, the underside of his chin next to you. This prevents him biting.
8. Tap LIGHTLY on the buttocks but on the same spot. This stings but does not bruise.
9. While this is going on, hold a conversation. He may start yelling. Ignore this. Inform Junior, in a quiet voice, he will tire of screaming before you tire of punishing him. "I am prepared to keep you here until you decide not to defy me". Tap, tap, tap. "I'll be good, I'll be good". "Do you really mean that?" Tap, tap, tap. Continue in this manner until you are satisfied Junior is aware you are not prepared to put up with his non-sense.
10. Afterwards he will go away and lick his wounds of humility and later apologise. Or he will lie on is back and kick and scream in an endeavour to convince you he has won. — Well! – You grab him by the scruff of his breeks and say "I see you have not had enough." The result is electric! YOU HAVE NO FURTHER PROBLEMS – EVER!!

I AM PERFECTLY AWARE THAT CORPORAL PUNISHMENT IS FROWNED UPON, BUT THIS METHOD DOES NOT CAUSE MENTAL OR PHYSICAL DAMAGE TO THE CHILD. There has never been a child born, nor ever will be, who does not, at some time, need corporal punishment. WHAT IS THE ALTERNATIVE??? Glue sniffing, drug use, worse still – drug dealers, fraudsters and so on and so on. – Given the opportunity without deterrent. Are you, as parents or guardians prepared to accept the responsibility for the actions of these children?

So many parents, mothers particularly, lose their authority because they are under the impression that if disobedience and defiance are ignored the problem will solve itself. DO NOT BE FOOLED. The longer you put off coping with the problem it grows more serious as the child grows older. The situation can be so serious that deprivation of goodies or loss of privilege have no effect. On reaching this desperate state either parent is CAPABLE OF LASHING OUT without thinking and BATTERING THE CHILD. Boxing the ears can cause permanent deafness. There can be brain damage, cigarette burns etc. etc. All these are criminal offences. THIS IS WHY I have taken so much trouble and care to explain in detail how to administer discipline and corporal punishment.

In the case of the very young these transgressions are usually committed in the mother's presence. You may deal with it at once. Do not postpone punishment until your husband returns. Don't forget young memories are short.

When the child has reached the age of seven years plus the mother may have to call on the intervention of the father, depending on the size and strength of the mother. So be it! But before punishment is administered a full explanation and discussion is required with the mother ON HER OWN with the father. Then with the child and both parents. FATHERS – READ THE INSTRUCTIONS ON ADMINISTRATION AND DO NOT OVERLOOK YOUR STRENGTH.

Once the child has experienced discipline and corporal punishment, when threatened he will talk! and perhaps give a legitimate reason for his action. DO NOT FORGET we are all human! Even children, (no matter how young), feel it is worth running the gauntlet!

READ ALL THIS CAREFULLY. It is intended to keep you out of court because of battered children. I have already dealt with battered babies.

Ask, order, threaten, act PREVENTS you losing your temper, retains your authority and the love and respect of your child.

In this day and age a child requires and NEEDS authorative and loving parents. These parents are the bastions for their children against glue sniffing, drugs, prostitution, stealing and bad company. EVERYTHING DEPENDS ON YOU, PARENTS! DO NOT FAIL your children.

BEFORE MARRIAGE

ADVICE TO PARENTS AND GRAND-PARENTS ETC.

1. Do not allow OR offer the Young Marrieds to share your home, whether they are paying guests or otherwise.
2. Grand-parents are usually the most vulnerable as a second choice as they may have a spare room.
3. INSIST on suitable independent living arrangements being made before marriage.
4. DO NOT go back on your word.
5. INSTILL into the young couple BEFORE marriage your attitude to living in.

Do not allow, or offer, the young marrieds accommodation. It is the worst thing for the young and parents alike. Lives can be shattered as you already know from the experience of others. I can hear you say "My child is different!" Perhaps so, but you did not marry their partner. That is the crunch! When circumstances have reached this desperate stage all is lost. Few families, if any, return to normal relationships after this traumatic experience.

When the child leaves school or college and becomes interested in the opposite sex this subject must be periodically referred to.

Do not harp on the subject but make remarks about starting to save, or not getting too serious before both have some security behind them. Ignore a curt reply. With regular reference to the subject the message will be received and understood.

A very important point; do not reverse your attitude towards living in no matter what the circumstances! The older people are always the ones hurt. You run the risk of your home and everything being taken from you. You must accept that once they are married they are totally independent and whether they plan to live in a house or sleep under a bridge is entirely their responsibility.

Emotion on your part must be overcome. The emotion of the parents towards their children is different to the emotions of children towards their parents. What must be realised is that your child has found a partner to replace the deeper dependence on you.

You can only advise, not insist, no matter how foolish the young may be. But! – you are in a position to insist the young ones do not return to live with you or their grand-parents. They may be displeased with your refusal but that is up to them, isn't it? In time life will return to normal and the relationship will not be broken for ever.

§

92

TO THE PARENTS/GUARDIANS WHEN THE YOUNG ARE LIVING-IN

1. Do not allow the Young Marrieds to take over your home.
2. Insist the young pay their full share of current expenses, including wear and tear.
3. Realise, BEFORE it is too late, there is no sentiment in business.

Perhaps by the time you read this your young-marrieds are already living in your home. You may be one of the few lucky ones whose lives are not disrupted. Long may it reign! More than likely you fall into the category of total disruption. Your home is bursting at the seams and ready to fall apart while the Young Marrieds grumble incessantly but continue to ride dry shot over you all.

1939 saw the birth of the "Shot Gun" wedding and, of course, no accommodation. During this period in World War II, there existed parental control and things worked out. Since 1950 too much spending money and increased leisure time has resulted in the decrease of this control as observed by terrorism, muggings and the like and the situation is worsening.

It can be deducted from this statement that parents must develop courage and determination. If you have any reason at all to be dissatisfied you must amend the conditions of living in. I say amend, as there may be very few conditions laid down, if any!

Heated argument may or will develop. Do not tolerate this. Is it your home. Should this hostile attitude persist the order is OUT!!! MEAN WHAT YOU SAY. I warned you; it takes great courage on the part of both parents. All unpleasant decisions take courage. We all like to be popular but not at that price! The Young marrieds will either pack up and go or will decide to abide by the rules. Whatever the outcome, peace will reign once more. They may not apologise. In this day and age it is a sign of defeat.

What I have written also applies to the single girls with infants.

§

93

TO THE YOUNG

1. The home belongs to your parents or guardians.
2. Once in receipt of salary, wages or social security, YOU BECOME a paying guest.
3. Your first consideration is towards your hosts (parents, guardians or grandparents), NOT yourselves or your young family.
4. You MUST be prepared to pay your FULL SHARE of expenses.
5. Should these rules prove irksome - GET OUT! find alternative accommodation.
6. The cost of alternative accommodation will certainly be higher than living in, - but that is up to you. ABIDE BY THE RULES.

What the majority of you young people (married or single) fail to realise is that when you earn a salary, wage or social security your parents' financial responsibilities cease. You become a guest, paying or otherwise, in your parents' home and you are expected to act as such.

Your parents' wishes, and those of your brothers and sisters, are the first to be considered NOT those of yourselves and of your young family. For instance, the baby's nappies must not be dried draped around the fire to the exclusion of everyone else. Of course they must be dried! but how about purchasing an adequate number to allow for wet days? or have packets of disposable nappies taking up every spare space of the living room. Talking about the fire - don't take possession of the most comfortable chair at every opportunity. Remember these seats are no longer yours by right. This is no longer your home. Another point – it is not necessary to use the kitchen and the cooker when your parents require the use of both and, worse still, using your husband and family as the excuse (refer to Weaning – Article no. 68). This may mean you having a late meal – so what? It won't kill either of you. Your children's meal times can be adjusted accordingly. It matters little what hours the child or baby is fed, so long as the hours are regular. These points will help to retain a pleasant atmosphere.

IT IS ESSENTIAL YOU PAY YOUR FULL EXPENSES. Yourselves and two children count as FOUR regardless of age. Four siblings, regardless of age, plus parents count as six. Total members of the house hold is TEN. (I am aware that this, in an ordinary household, is gross overcrowding, but I am using the number to illustrate a point.) ALL BILLS, (electricity, gas, water etc) are divided by ten. You pay 3/5 of all these accounts PLUS an ADEQUATE RENT, whether you like it or not!

Should you dislike ANY of these arrangements, COMMENCE looking for other accommodation. DO NOT say you are unable to find a place! What you mean is – there is no other place so cheap! More expensive accommodation will cut into your standard of living, smoking, drinking, holidays... At least you have these items on which to economise.

Your parents are usually the best friends you will ever have. Make sure you do not lose this relationship through your selfishness, stubborness and stupidity. Do think hard before disrupting their home by allowing your family to destroy the furniture with sticky fingers, running around without nappies, treading food into the carpets AND damaging door posts and furniture with pram wheels.

The state of the parents' furniture and fittings must be in the same condition when you leave as when you took up residence. They built up a comfortable home for themselves, NOT for you to destroy.

THE BUDGET

94

LIST FOR THE BUDGET

		1	2	3	4	5
1.	TOTAL INCOME					
2.	Mortgage					
3.	Rent					
4.	Community Charge					
5.	Water Rates					
6.	Gas					
7.	Electricity					
8.	Oil					
9.	Coal					
10.	Telephone					
11.	External maintenance					
12.	Decorating					
13.	Replacements					
14.	Clothes					
15.	Cosmetics etc					
16.	Christmas Gifts					
17.	Christmas fare					
18.	Christmas Cards					
19.	Birthday Presents					
20.	Birthday Cards					
	total					
	CARRY FORWARD					

139

		1	2	3	4	5
	BROUGHT FORWARD					
21.	Postage					
22.	Holidays					
23.	Sickness					
24.	Insurances (total)					
25.	Prescription Charges .					
26.	Car replacement					
27.	Car maintenance					
28.	Television Licence . .					
39.	Television Rental . . .					
30.	Hire Purchase . . . . . . (until paid off)					
31.	Travelling Expenses .					
32.	Night school fees					
33.	Night school exp. . . .					
34.	School Meals					
35.	Food					
36.	Savings $1/2$ of 2nd . . . (income)					
37.	Any Other Expenses .					
	GRAND TOTAL					

I have drawn up a comprehensive list for budgeting. Not all items apply to everyone, for instance Mortgage/Rent. It is rather frightening when you study this list and realise how far an income must stretch!

Sometimes both of you are working. IGNORE the lesser income. Be very strong minded about this. Save it. Should the day arrive when there is one income and you have budgeted for two, you could land in debt overnight. Use $1/2$ the lesser income if you must but only to repay hire purchase. NEVER USE ALL. Once the HP is paid off SAVE THAT AMOUNT.

REGULARLY invest the second income in Account No 3 of the

Building Society. This is your nest egg. It will gain interest which can be withdrawn IF YOU MUST. Preferably leave it to gain compound interest (interest on the interest).

Copy the comprehensive list PLUS the spaces onto a squared paper. In the first column write against each item the amount YOU THINK YOU'LL REQUIRE for the year ahead. When added up the total will PROBABLY be TWICE the amount of your annual income! The remaining columns will be necessary for adjusting your expenditure to suit your income. THIS IS CALLED CHEESE-PARING! A VERY DIFFICULT PROCESS. The lower the income the more difficult it is to accomplish. the longer it takes to balance the budget, the greater the necessity for cheese-paring – and care when spending.

I have written pages on Important Information about the budget (Nos 98-135) containing advice on each item on the budget list.

Reading it through all at once may prove rather heavy going. You will not get your budget balanced in one day or two (more likely two weeks to four). I suggest as you sort out each item, you turn to the Important Information pages and read what I have written about the subject.

Some of you may decide the task is beyond you. Do not be afraid to ask for help of an intelligent trusted friend or relation. They may be inclined to think you mad! Do not be side-tracked by their lack of enthusiasm. Insist on their help! By the time they have finished with you they may contemplate embarking on a similar scheme.

Make certain the total is correct. It is surprising how many different answers one can arrive at. Have it checked and RECHECKED. You cannot afford to make a mistake.

Once the final total has been ascertained divide it; by 12 if in receipt of a salary; by 52 if a wage earner. Pay the amount arrived at regularly into the building society and ask for a cheque to pay the bills. This account (Account No 1) is to be used ONLY FOR YOUR HOUSE-HOLD EXPENDITURE. It will earn interest which can be drawn out each year and transferred to another account for saving.

The food allowance (including cleaning materials) is kept to hand on a weekly or monthly basis and spent as required. Make sure you do not overspend.

Keep an accurate record of money spent on all items included in the budget list. AVOID slipping the change into your housekeeping purse. This change is vital and is part of your tight budget. Have a separate purse or container for the change. This expenditure list acts as a guide for the following year's budget.

You may have very little money to spend on yourselves – but the day will come when you shall. The hard time spent with tight budgeting and deprivation will reap its reward.

NB. keep your expenses low, even if your income is increased. If you learn to live on a little you can always live on a lot!

BUILDING SOCIETY ORDINARY SHARE ACCOUNTS

95

ACCOUNT No 1

This account is EXCLUSIVELY for your budget account. Depending on how your wage/salary is paid the same amount must be paid into this account regardless. At the end of your financial year transfer any surplus. For example, external maintenance and decorating and carry it forward to the next year. The remaining interest gained from the account, transfer to No 3 account.

I can hear you say "That won't be worth much" but just you wait and see! Do not be alarmed when your fuel bill, mortgage or insurance etc. increase. As they increase the money earns more interest for you in this account. At least this is some compensation. Had you been paying bills as they came in, just out of your pocket, all this interest would have been lost due to lack of investment.

Pay as many bills as possible with building society cheques.

§

ACCOUNT No 2

This account is A MUST if you run a car. Presume you will replace the car in 5 years. A ¹/5 of the cost MUST be paid in ANNUALLY IN WEEKLY/MONTHLY installments. No interest must be withdrawn, the interest copes with the increased cost of another car.

It is preferable to pay the car tax and insurance into this account. Again in weekly/monthly installments. I would like to draw your attention to the fact that the initial purchase of a car is the cheapest part of the operation.

ALWAYS PAY BY BUILDING SOCIETY CHEQUE.

ACCOUNT No 3 – (Your Nest Egg)

Should you both be working, at least half, preferably the whole, of the LESSER income should be paid into this account. This ensures that when only one is employed you have been used to working on only one income. Your security remains intact!

This account may mean the deposit for your home, failing that at least the beginning of your nest egg. This account also holds the interest gained from your budget account (No 1).

Interest may be withdrawn from this account when necessary but you lose COMPOUND interest. This interest is paid on interest. Over the years it amounts to a lot of money.

The money in this account can also be used as collateral (security for borrowing from the bank for an overdraft). You may borrow the amount in the book with approximately £25.00 expenses to cover costs. Arrangements are made with the bank manager regarding your rate of repayment of the overdraft. HP companies who state their terms regardless of your inability to pay are very tempting. DO NOT BE FOOLED. Overdrafts are expensive, the repayment interest is high. HP is higher! But there is one consolation, this No 3 Account is still earning for your compound interest during the period of repaying the overdraft.

Should you work overtime, use the income to repay your overdraft. HP does not allow this especially when the repayments are irregular. All the time you have an overdraft you are losing money but not as much as on HP.

All through this budget no doubt you have noticed I have not included allowances for smoking, drinking or gambling. While balancing your budget you will realise there is no money for such frivolities. Indeed you have just realised just how poor you are! Calculate how much you spend on these items per week. Add them together then multiply the total by 52. The amount is staggering!

No one can make you save! It is good budgeting, the urge to do so and SELF DISCIPLINE.

REMEMBER!!....YOU CAN ONLY SPEND MONEY ONCE!!

Some of the surplus after the budget calculations may be divided by two – pocket money for each. There is no reason why one should be entitled to more than the other.

IMPORTANT INFORMATION
– THE BUDGET

98

THE MORTGAGE
(Account No 1)

When you purchase your own home mortgage is paid instead of rent. The repayments can fluctuate these days according to the rise and fall of the interest rates. When there is a change in the interest rates the building society informs the mortgagee (yourself) as to whether there is a preference to an increase on monthly repayments OR to retain the present rate of repayment and EXTEND the borrowing time. DO TRY TO INCREASE PAYMENTS. Your detailed list for the budget (No 92) is the deciding factor depending on how generous you have been towards your Overheads allowance. Should this allowance not be capable of absorbing the extra payment unfortunately there is no option but to continue as before and extend the time of borrowing.

When the repayment period is completed you have paid the building society approximately TWICE the purchasing value of the house. The extended period of repayment makes it even more than twice. BUT at least you have a home.

Shop around – terms very. Your solicitor and Building Society can advise you. Before you decide on any repayment plan read article No. 138.

99

RENT
(Account No 1)

This is really throwing good money after bad! But at least it is better than Living in. At least you have made the effort. Depending on how you pay your rent ALWAYS PAY BY CHEQUE. Your building society will issue one on request.

Some landlords are rather unscrupulous. They fail to issue rent books. Whatever happens a cheque is proof of payment. REFUSE TO PAY RENT IN CASH. If cash is demanded get legal advice.

§

100

COUNCIL TAX
(Account No 1)

This is not included in the rent. NEVER, NEVER, pay by installments. The council COLLECTS ALL THE INTEREST at your expense. You are not given a discount. Pay this money into your No 1 account AGAIN request the building society to issue a cheque when payment is due, once or twice a year.

101

WATER CHARGES
(Account No 1)

These may be included in the rent – though increasingly, they are likely to be separate. If they are separate DO NOT PAY BY INSTALL-MENTS. Invest the money in No 1 Account and pay by cheque, once or twice a year.

§

102

GAS
(Account No 1)

You may use this fuel for cooking, hot water, heating, or all three. Ask a relative or friend who uses gas in the same way as yourself, to advise you regarding the cost over the period of a year. AGAIN and again I say DO NOT be talked into paying by installments. Ask the building society for a cheque.

When a slot meter (if installed) is due to be emptied, pay the amount used in treasury notes or by cheque and ask for the coins to be returned for future use. This makes life easier – no hunting for coins!

ELECTRICITY
(Account No 1)

All the instructions for the use of gas are applicable for the use of electricity. It is easier to waste electricity than gas, so take care. Do not leave the hot tap running to no purpose, eg washing odd plates; use a bowl. An immersion heater switches on and off without you being aware of it. It is the most extravagant and so the most expensive item in the house. The ELECTRICITY COMPANIES issue leaflets informing you of the approximate running costs of various electrical appliances. Of course use what you require but DO NOT WASTE. You feather the nests of the Electricity Companies at the expense of your own.

Always use ADEQUATE lighting. The cost is negligible in comparison with other appliances. A reminder: NO PAYMENT BY INSTALL-MENTS.

§

104

OIL
(Account No 1)

This is a clean, convenient fuel and was reasonably cheap. It fell from favour due to the rapid rise in cost of oil. If the price again becomes reasonable it may regain its popularity. Oil is primarily used in isolated areas where there is no gas. It is very convenient in the form of central heating and Aga-type cookers, for the elderly and disabled. It is regularly serviced by the individual firms. There is always a warm oven, which saves the purchase of pressure cookers or slow cookers etc. There is always a hot plate for boiling, simmering, toasting and, of course, a warm room, hot water and central heating - if so desired.

It is difficult to advise regarding running costs. Advice can be obtained from an oil firm or a "Consumer" heating firm. Economy is an art which has to be learnt. There is a great deal to be said in favour of oil! Taking into account the costs of alternative fuels there is, in all probability, little difference in running costs. AGAIN do enter into an installment plan.

§

105

COAL (Account No 1)

Smokeless fuel is about the only solid fuel available these days, and is certainly not the cheapest nor the most convenient. There are slow combustion burners available but these have to be fitted *professionally* – NO DIY workmanship; no matter how tempting financially. The majority of these slow combustion burners only require attention twice daily but when looking after the elderly or the sick this can prove demanding and therefore inconvenient. There are more suitable alternatives.

§

106

TELEPHONE (Account No 1)

While living-in you may have the use of your parent's telephone. The telephone is always a bone of contention. For example, if the household consists of a total of ten people (including children of all ages) the telephone bill is divided by 10. Say the account is £40.60. The living-in family – consisting of yourselves and two children – must pay £4.06 x 4. This amounts to £16.24.

If you object to this method and cause unpleasantness your parents have a perfect right to refuse you access. They may consider a lock on the telephone which prevents OUT going calls. Using a kiosk is more expensive and not so convenient. Your parents, may decide to invest in a "Pay Phone" and THAT will cut out ALL ARGUMENTS!

EXTERNAL MAINTENANCE
(Account No 1)

After asking advice be as generous as you can. External maintenance is self explanatory. do not ignore this care. Replacement is far more expensive. It must take priority to decoration, fitted kitchen and other luxuries. Do not forget the roof in your calculations. Painting requires full maintenance EVERY 3 years. Therefore 1/3 of the total cost must be paid into the No 1 account EACH year; and that is for painting alone. The important factor is just how do you intend to carry out this maintenance? Do you intend to undertake this work yourself? Are you versed in the correct techniques and pitfalls? The lack of knowledge could prove expensive. If you decide against DIY make sure you engage a reputable firm. STEER CLEAR OF THE COWBOY, be he your friend or someone elses. They are not insured against accidents or poor workmanship. Ask to inspect a local house he has worked on and get references. BEFORE finally engaging someone, enquire as to whether they hold a comprehensive insurance. DEMAND PROOF! If not satisfied, bow out gracefully. IT IS YOUR MONEY THAT IS BEING SPENT. You may be legally liable for accidents such as falling off ladders or roofs resulting in serious injury.

Carry forward maintenance in hand from year to year. Keep a record of the amount you spend and the balance. When an expensive repair rears its head your budgeting is adequate. DO NOT REDUCE THE AMOUNT PAID INTO YOUR ACCOUNT for maintenance, no matter how tempted. Should you move house in the future you will be pleased to discover there are sufficient funds accumulated for immediate repairs to your new home. KEEP ALL RECEIPTS INDEFINITELY – in case you emigrate! – for example. There is such a thing called CAPITAL GAINS TAX. These receipts are required to reduce or eliminate this tax.

DECORATING
(Account No 1)

This means just what it says but it also includes rewiring and plumbing. After rewiring there is always a large decorating bill. I refer to plumbing mainly because of frozen pipes, radiators etc. The insurance covers decoration and damage to furniture and furnishings but NOT REPAIRS to pipes.

The majority of young people are capable of undertaking their own decorating. The result may not be 100% but at least the place looks cared for and clean. One family informed me that it proved more economical for a PROFESSIONAL firm to advise and undertake the work. It lasts longer and looks expensive (which it is). It is worth bearing in mind, especially when very expensive materials are used.

Decorating is one of the items which lends itself to economy. If you are really pushed for money it can be skipped. The ceiling may get blacker and blacker and the wallpaper more faded as time goes on. DO NOT go into debt by overspending on this item. At least your home is wind and water tight AND THAT IS WHAT COUNTS.

Should anyone pass remarks about the condition of the decoration, your answer is "You purchase the wallpaper, paint and other necessities and get on with the job at your own expense." There will never be another word said. It is entirely your business and that of no one else.

Similar to external maintenance – keep a check on expenditure and carry forward the balance to each successive year.

REPLACEMENTS
(Account No 1)

How often this ordinary heading hides a multitude of sins! Broken mugs, worn out sheets, towels, tea towels, shoe repairs, shoe laces, teaspoons which have a habit of disappearing. The list is endless. The "Food" allowance is not sufficient to cope. What is left over from those replacement allowance should be carried forward from year to year and a record kept in the same way as decorating and external maintenance.

§

110

OVERHEADS
(Account No 1)

How many times have you heard someone say "I have no money to spare, what on earth am I going to do!!" Well, the overheads cover the "Unexpected". A journey to a sick relative, rise in Council Tax, fuel etc. A journey to a sick relative MUST be made but it takes money. A rise in mortgage or Council Tax MUST be paid; again extra money is required. Not to mention wedding presents. Without getting into an awful muddle, you are unable to borrow from any "Item". It is ONLY the Overheads that cater for the unexpected. Be as generous as possible when working out your annual budget. The Overheads is your safety valve. Any money left over at the end of the year; carry it forward to your next budget (no matter how little) but make a note of it.

111

CLOTHES
(Account No 1)

One can spend a fortune on clothes or virtually nothing. At least one of your items that can be culled to make ends meet.

I presume you have been spending a considerable amount of your wages on clothes, or perhaps your unemployment benefit – thanks to your parents' generosity! My advice is to refrain from purchasing way-out clothes. They have a habit of going out of fashion.

When funds are low Charity shops/Car Boot Sales (good ones) are an excellent source of supply, especially if you learn the art of dressmaking and alterations. Always carry a tape measure. The Next to New shops are good but more expensive. In some areas children's clothes and uniforms are sold in Church and Village Halls. There are wonderful bargains. At least in this day and age there are jumble sales. In the 1920s and 1930s there was no such thing! No one parted with clothes capable of being cut down to size and worn. After that the seams were unpicked, clothes were washed, cut up into strips and used to make "Clippy Mats" - excellent for stone or concrete floors!

§

112

COSMETICS
(Account No 1)

This includes perms, shampoo and sets, trims, and any form of make up, not forgetting shaving soap, after shave, deoderants, talc etc.

Approximately 25% of lipsticks, eyeshadows and other cosmetics are wasted in the holders; USE IT ALL.

Cut tubes such as toothpastes with scissors - you will be surprised how much is left behind after the "Last Squeeze" Perhaps you know all about that without me spelling it out – but it does save money.

113

CHRISTMAS GIFTS
(Account No 1)

Even if you are affluent it is a mistake to purchase expensive gifts at this
time of the year, regardless of the recipient, especially for children.
There is so much distraction during this period expensive gifts are not
appreciated. After all, Christmas gifts are only a token. A good rule to
remember: the recipient is usually unaware you have seen the more
expensive gift. A child loves variety and surprises – there is no time for
concentration and appreciation. Small wrapped gifts are ideal. A
favourite present for a seven year old girl was a pretty box containing a
home made hair decoration, a pen and a bar of chocolate! As the child
becomes older the value of gifts may increase within limits. Beginning
with expensive gifts when young the sky is the limit by the time the
child is a teenager or before.

§

114

CHRISTMAS FARE
(Account No 1)

Your food/housekeeping allowance certainly will not allow for the extra
entertaining and the general Christmas fare. This must be budgeted for.
try to keep within your budget limits. Endeavour to make the most of
the goodies yourself – mince meat, mince pies, Christmas cake, ice-
cream, fruit drinks and more. They taste much nicer and usually prove
cheaper.

115

CHRISTMAS CARDS AND BIRTHDAY CARDS
(Account No 1)

These I feel, cost an awful lot of money just to be eventually torn up and thrown in the dustbin. Think first before you buy. Many of you with time and patience, are capable of making wonderful cards for very little cost. Certainly encourage children to make their own greeting cards. Your relations and friends will appreciate the time and effort spent. Do not overlook the cost of postage. It can be unexpectedly staggering, especially at Christmas. Buy Christmas cards – wrapping paper – immediately after Christmas when they are often sold for half price.

§

116

POSTAGE
(Account No 1)

I can hear you saying "Oh, I never write letters!" That may be true, to a point, but everyone must post something sometime: Christmas Cards, Birthday Cards, gifts, business letters, not forgetting overseas mail and holiday postcards. At times the postage exceeds the value of the package. Whatever the amount you arrive at, include it in your budget. No longer is it an item to be ignored!

117

BIRTHDAY GIFTS

(Account No 1)

It is advisable to spend the greater portion of Gift Money on birthday gifts. Of course this is purely a matter of opinion. Children are in a position to appreciate a more expensive gift on that day away from Christmas festivities.

Think in advance; purchase gifts during sales.

§

118

HOLIDAYS

(Account No 1)

All I can say about this is MAKE CERTAIN the insurance offered by the travel agency is ADEQUATE for your requirements. There is so much cut-throat competition, with cowboys thrown in. These package holidays can prove disastrous unless you have money to spare should you require it. Book through a travel agent who is a member of ABTA – you are covered if the operator's company collapses. Do check whether or not your travel agent offers money-back guarantee, should it be necessary.

So many of these firms are good at bending the truth. A visit to a solicitor is worth-while. To spend a few pounds to check over insurance and terms is cheaper than having things go wrong. Should you, in spite of precautions, be unlucky, at least you have a solicitor who is familiar with your case. Consider a separate travel insurance and make sure it will get you home and meet any extra costs. Pay by building society cheque is proof of payment. Do not use a credit card in case you are still away when payment is due. – Interest is very high. There are so many stories of food-poisoning, accidents and unforeseen bills; it is a case of Buyer beware.

On a tight budget, I am sure you'll agree, holidays as such, are not really a necessity. There is no cheaper holiday than staying at home. NOT galavanting every day but putting your feet up and relaxing without worry, because your precious money remains in your pocket. Galavanting every day can prove equally expensive as an organised holiday. Your parents/friends would willingly have your children if not for a whole week to sleep, at least daily. (Hence the title of this book!) No grand-parent will refuse well behaved children. Do not forget to hand over money for food and other expenses. To have grand-children without parents fussing around can prove a great joy to both children and grand-parents alike.

A holiday at home if approached in the correct manner, that is not being disgruntled because the situation has been forced upon you, will prove more restful and beneficial than the usual type of holiday. More important – you will have time to talk – to discuss your life, your work, your pleasures, your problems, each others relations (especially in-laws), and, very important, your plans for the future. Understanding and patience, including tolerance, is the natural outcome of talking and listening. The result is strength to face the future no matter what difficulties life has in store for you.

119
SICKNESS
(Account No 1)

Some terms of employment do not allow for the continuance of wages while off sick. No work, no pay! – only NHS Benefit. It is better than nothing but it complicates your No 1 account and this you cannot afford to do. I suggest you budget for three weeks wages per year. Should you be lucky enough not to be off sick or unemployed, carry this money forward to the next year. still continue to pay these three weeks "Sick Money" into your No 1 account. Gradually you will build up a sum of money to cope with a long-term illness or unemployment.

This could be paid through an insurance policy. The snag is – should you, by luck or good fortune, not be off sick or unemployed during the year, you LOSE YOUR MONEY! Provided you can be sufficiently strong minded to include it in your budget. DO NOT BE TEMPTED to withdraw any of it just because you have not been off work. In about three or four years, providing none of this money has been used, you may then pay three weeks into your PERMANENT SAVINGS ACCOUNT (Account No 3).

§

120
INSURANCE
(Account No 1)

A vast subject but a very important one – SO READ CAREFULLY. ALWAYS USE THE SERVICES OF AN INSURANCE BROKER NEVER AN AGENT WHO COLLECTS REGULARLY AT YOUR DOOR.

An insurance broker is specially trained and belongs to the SOCI-ETY OF INSURANCE BROKERS. These people deal with MANY insurance companies. All these insurance companies have their own specialities and special offers. The insurance broker will be at liberty to choose the particular company best fitted for your own special needs. He can alter your insurance company any time when another company offers a better deal. This is certainly an advantage. This may happen often, especially in car insurance which is very competitive. Using a Broker costs no more than going direct to an insurance company.

§

121

INSURANCE AGENT

The agent works EXCLUSIVELY for ONE particular insurance company. Regardless of terms offered he is UNABLE to ALTER your policy from one company to another.

TO PAY ANNUALLY IS LESS EXPENSIVE than by installments.

§

122

THE HOUSE AND BUILDINGS
(Account No 1)

Your building society INSISTS your property is insured with their own choice of insurance company. Insist it is a Comprehensive insurance and on an INCREASE VALUATION BASIS. This means as the value of your property increases you are sent an increased payment demand. Some companies do this automatically OTHERS DON'T and leave the decision in your hands. Time passes THEN WHAM! The house goes on fire or is vandalised. It is then you discover, to your cost, you are UNDER INSURED!! AND THEN WHAT??

Some companies include lightening, flood, riots and so forth. Some may not. This is where the services of an insurance broker is so valuable. If you fail to understand what it is all about, ASK, ASK, AND ASK AGAIN. Failing that take someone with you who can understand and help you to ask the right questions. IT IS YOUR MONEY THAT

IS BEING SPENT AND IT IS YOUR HOME THAT MUST BE INSURED. Make sure you understand what it is all about BEFORE you sign on the dotted line. Mistakes have a habit to drift on and then there can be tragedy.

§

123

HOUSE CONTENTS
(Account No 1)

At first you may have no idea where to begin! Begin with pricing each article of furniture, jewellery, household equipment, tools etc. in EACH room. Make a list and note the price you paid for each item and date of purchase. KEEP RECEIPTS. If you are unable to price an item go around the shops until you find something similar, note the cost and the date seen.

Any article of furniture or anything given to you by an elderly person, visit a reputable dealer to give you some idea of its value. A photograph is helpful. Do not destroy the photograph. DO NOT visit (friend or otherwise) round the corner who owns a junk shop.

When you have completed your list, purchase a decent cash book. Enter date of purchase, description, registration marks, and purchase price. AGAIN I say negotiate with an insurance broker. Produce your cash book PLUS photographs. Discuss the value of any goods purchased at a house sale, such as curtains or blankets, usually of excellent quality. you may have got them for a song but to replace after a fire or burglary in the same quality would cost a bomb!

Take the complete list also copies of photographs to the insurance broker. Request he makes a copy for himself. Add to the list the purchase of later goods. this is VERY IMPORTANT. In case of fire or burglary you have a list of everything you possess plus photographs, making life much easier for yourself, the police and the insurance company.

1. Have a comprehensive insurance policy.
2. Make certain it includes a phrase REPLACE AS NEW in all circumstances.

3. Add to your list and that of the brokers as you purchase goods.
4. Have your antiques adequately valued.
5. Have a cost of living increase AUTOMATICALLY added to your premium.

Do not grudge the insurance; pay it no matter what you do without.

You youngsters possess the goods burglars want. Disposal is easy because of demand. There is no need to spell it out! In this day and age the demand for drugs demands easy money. — Burglary!

§

124
LIFE ASSURANCE
(Account No 1)

A good idea but do not bite off more than you can chew, as the saying goes! should you ever be unable to continue payments the life assurance becomes void and you lose your money, or the most of it, UNLESS you have been sufficiently prudent to pay each year into your No 1 Account your three weeks "Sickness" money to cover payments when off sick or unemployed.

At the beginning of your adult life this insurance is not vital. It can easily be arranged at a later date when your finances are on a firmer footing. The lower the age the lower the cost.

125
CAR
(Account No 2)

I presume you have a car – I may be wrong! – The majority of you young folk have. I am also sure you purchased a reasonable car on hire purchase or a very old banger for cash.

If you run a car you must afford to do so adequately. It is much more expensive than you think. This account is only used to *replace* the car.

Running costs of a car.

1. The initial cost of the car.
2. REPLACEMENT of vehicle (5 years) or on account of accident, write off or wear and tear.
3. Running costs – petrol and oil.
4. Servicing - the type you are unable to cope with – ALSO MOT.
5. Road Licence (Tax)
6. Insurance.
7. Excess on insurance claim.
8. Spare parts – INCLUDING tyres (30,000 miles).
9. Annual total mileage.
10. AA/RAC cover.

A car is really a luxury, not a necessity, unless your work demands unsociable hours; working in a hospital or an airport. A motorcycle is cheaper. Using the car for work DEMANDS full comprehensive insurance; this includes the HIRE of a car should the need arise. This is essential when depending on the car for work. Failing that, you could become unemployed on account of poor attendance due to breakdowns.

ALWAYS pay the salesman or the HP Company by cheque issued by your building society. NEVER CASH. Once the full HP is paid CONTINUE to pay monthly into Account No 2 for the eventual REPLACEMENT of the car (5 years).

Keep a DETAILED account of every expense on the car. Also keep a daily record of mileage for work and pleasure. Your work mileage may be allowed by the firm for travelling expenses; (the reason for a separate mileage record). All running expenses and maintenance is

162

catered for in Account No 1.

Another interesting point is an accident repair may prove cheaper than forfeiting your insurance "No Claims" bonus. Make enquiries before you decide. Providing you have been paying an adequate amount in addition to the replacement of the car to cover garage bills, MOT and tyres there will be no problem. (The petrol and oil is included in the travelling expenses.) Hence the regular paying in to your car account (Account No 2).

§

126
TV LICENCE
(Account No 1)

This, as do all other items listed in the Budget Account, earns money for you. Again I advise you not to purchase stamps to cover the licence. YOU LOSE YOUR INTEREST as the Post Office FAILS to give you a discount.

§

127
TV RENTALS
(Account No 1)

Paying rental annually is cheaper than monthly payments as this money earns interest for you. Rent your TV from a REPUTABLE private firm rather than a national company. After several years they may be prepared to sell the set to you with good after-sales service. Continue to pay your "Rental" into your budget account. This will cover costs of repairs and ultimately a new set. These private firms are very jealous of their reputation. Pay by the building society cheque.

128
HIRE PURCHASE
(Account No 3)

THE MILL STONE THAT GRINDS THE LIFE OUT OF YOU AND THROWS ONE INTO THE DUST. It is the cause of getting deeper and deeper into debt, the break up of marriages, humiliation when goods are reclaimed, excessive drinking – drinking which those in debt can ill-afford – and, of course, money lenders. You name it – HP can cause it! If cash is short AVOID CREDIT CARDS LIKE THE PLAGUE. This is a sophisticated way of going to the money-lenders. REPAYMENT INTEREST IS VERY HIGH.

The catalogues are a great temptation with glossy attractive pictures. Steer clear! Instead, keep your eyes open for notices in the newspapers for auctions or house sales. (I do not mean "House Parties".) These sales are often held in large houses or auction rooms. The owner has died and the house effects are to be sold. Make a list of everything you require and the measurements. ALWAYS carry a tape measure. There is a viewing day when everything is open for inspection before being bundled up for auction. The men wandering around in overalls (auctioneer's assistants) have a shrewd idea of the selling price. Ask their advice and write down their price. Until you become experienced I advise you NOT TO GO BEYOND THEIR PRICE. BUT ALWAYS REMEMBER there are OTHER FISH IN THE SEA AND OTHER OPPORTUNITIES. There is commission to pay on these goods. Even if you only window shop at these sales and attend them without bidding, you will learn how to bid. It is an art! Once you have acquired it you are on the band wagon. You will find it absorbing. Should you be disappointed in an article you purchased, return it to the sale room for auction. Also read every week the list of private sellers. One bit of advice, with furniture, LOOK OUT FOR WOODWORM. If it's a valuable piece of furniture a registered firm will treat it for you.

You MAY USE the second income to pay off the HP and NOT for anything else. Once you have paid off the HP, NEVER, NEVER, NEVER touch HP again. Put this money into your building society Account No 3 for PERMANENT SAVING.

REMEMBER, REMEMBER, HP is a VERY LUCRATIVE way of feathering other people's nests at the expense of your own!

129
TRAVELLING EXPENSES
(Account No 1)

The travelling expenses for the whole family are included, covering work, school, shopping trips, night school, school outings etc. You may think the odd 20p can easily come out of the housekeeping to cover travelling – this is a NO GO area.

When calculating this item jot down all the known expenses for the 12 months to allow as much as you can afford for increase of fares. Again if you fall short there is always the "OVERHEADS" to fall back on. I must draw your attention again the Overheads can only do what you allow them to do! Be as generous as you can with the allowances for overheads during your first year of budgeting.

§

130
NIGHT SCHOOL FEES
(Account No 1)

These have increased at an alarming rate. I suggest, for example, the boys may approach an upholsterer and the girls a tailor or dressmaker both with City and Guilds Qualifications. As a rule most craftsmen are unwilling to take on help in case redundancy has to be paid which they can ill afford. Give assurance you are prepared to work for travelling expenses only until you become efficient and experienced. It is cheaper than night school fees. Woodwork and soft furnishings may be done at night school; they are more suitable as night school subjects. A hairdressing course may also save money later.

When you become efficient in these subjects you have the means at your finger tips to make a comfortable home at reasonable cost.

131
NIGHT SCHOOL EXPENSES
(Account No 1)

The night school fees have been catered for, also the travelling expenses – I hope! but there are tools and materials to supply. The cost is rather difficult to assess, but assessments must be made for budgeting purposes.

Upholstery and tailoring are expensive trades, requiring expensive materials, a great deal of practice and personal supervision. This is why I suggested even working for nothing, except for travelling expenses.

These days or evening occupations prevent or discourage wasting your precious money on drinking and smoking. Most people can make a DIY cupboard or a cushion cover. Other home skills require private tuition or attendance at night school.

Reading this may flabbergast you! Working for nothing!!! Remember, you young people, for everything worth having in this life there is a price to pay. There are also rewards but only if the price is paid first. One reward – you will not be classed as one of these layabouts who will neither work nor do without. You will gain the admiration and respect of those who matter.

When you do get your own home, with these assets at your finger tips, given time, you can transform an otherwise humble abode into a miniature Buckingham Palace. All brought about by the use of your brains, your hands and your good will.

§

132
PRESCRIPTION CHARGES
(Account No 1)

Apart from prescription charges there are charges for dental treatment, spectacles, inoculations and vaccinations necessary for some over-seas countries. Try to allow an adequate amount for your budget. All these items are expensive so be realistic. Again, holidays at home are cheapest.

166

133
SCHOOL MEALS
(Account No 1)

Money for this item varies because of absenteeism and holidays. If you depend on the money to come out of the housekeeping some of you may find it difficult to cope. It would be sensible to give a flask of soup, some sliced meat, buttered wholemeal bread and some fruit. Use the disposable plastic cutlery. Should it get lost it is cheap and easy to replace.

It is no use making up packed lunches and then decide against it; you have slept in, lack of suitable food in the house, or lost interest. Your housekeeping allowance will not stretch to that sort of expenditure. It is advisable to budget and should you decide to pack a lunch it is a financial bonus.

§

134
FOOD
(Account No 1)

This money covers food, soaps, washing powders and cleaning materials ONLY. It is not necessary to keep a list of what you spend. "Convenient Foods"; crisps, ice-cream, sweets, juices, and other luxury items are very expensive. This is where your cookery course comes into its own. During the course ask advice about recycling of left over food and the title of a recommended book on the subject. If you must have ice-cream, make your own. Use the Public Library to browse through the cookery books.

135
BALANCING THE BUDGET

My Oh My!! I wonder just how long it has taken you to balance your budget using only one income. Perhaps I can guess! Using this method – I have done it all my working life and NOW I am reaping the reward. There is one thing certain, your efforts have made you realise just how poor you are.

At least the whole plan is constructive. As your household expenses increase (Account No 1), so does the interest increase which will be transferred annually to your Permanent Savings Account (No 3). As previously suggested purchase a decent diary and enter into it DAILY EACH ITEM OF EXPENDITURE AND THE AMOUNT spent on each. Items of food may be excluded as they, as a rule, remain static throughout the year, and are included in the weekly /monthly allowance

Do not be under the impression that within three or four years everything in the garden will be lovely – IT WON'T! but with patience and perseverance you have learnt the value of money and disciplined yourselves to say "No" to a spending spree.

Another point worth mentioning! It is easier to do without when young than in later life. YOUNG SPENDERS ARE WASTEFUL SPENDERS!

There is one golden rule NEVER spend capital but use the interest ONLY in a dire emergency. The only positive point about this: there is more interest to come from where that came from. The other side of the coin is there is less interest to come at the end of the year. EACH YEAR YOU WILL LOSE INTEREST on that interest you spent! This is the other way of appreciating compound interest. Again I say you can only spend your money once.

138
ENDOWMENT POLICY

You may purchase a house through an endowment policy. It has only ONE advantage – should the owner/occupier die, payments on the house cease and the dependent receives a lump sum and pays no further mortgage.

The other side of the coin is not so good. (1) You CANNOT reduce the years of repayment, even if you wish to. (2) Should your circumstances alter for the worse, THERE IS NO ADJUSTMENT OF REPAYMENTS. You could end up losing your home.

My advice: Do not purchase a house under the "Endowment Policy Plan". Take out an insurance policy if you wish but independent of the mortgage.

§

139
NOW FOR THE SNAGS

In the Endowment Scheme the monthly payments are higher than a straight forward mortgage as they include a Life Policy. DO NOT BE TEMPTED BY THIS METHOD. Difficulty obtaining a mortgage is usually because of too low an income. BUILDING SOCIETIES DO NOT MAKE MISTAKES! THINK! If you have difficulty paying a mortgage how on earth are you to manage on a still higher payment which includes the Life Insurance? THINK!

THINK, THINK! Repaying an ordinary mortgage you can increase payments after consultation with the building society and complete repayments before the allotted time. THIS IS IMPOSSIBLE WITH AN ENDOWMENT POLICY. You pay for the full time 20/25/30 years REGARDLESS OF CIRCUMSTANCES.

You may become permanently unemployed, sick or disabled. THE PAYMENTS must continue. YOU ARE IN DANGER OF LOSING your home and all or most of the money you have paid.

140
PRIVATE SURVEYOR

Always engage your own private surveyor even when purchasing council property. This may appear like throwing good money away. Don't you believe it! Should there be any structural faults etc. revealed as a result of the survey he may recommend a reduction in the selling price. The whys and wherefores he will discuss with you. Try not to be a "Know All" follow his advice and ask for a further explanation about anything you do not understand. Your own surveyor will PREVENT you falling into the trap of a second mortgage. I am aware the building society surveyor surveys the property but FOR THEIR BENEFIT NOT YOURS. Someone purchased council property (a private resale) without a private survey and later discovered it was full of woodworm.

NEVER, NEVER, NEVER borrow money for repairs or improvements, In case you do not realise it the repayment interest is VERY HIGH. Much higher than an ordinary mortgage.

I finish with the advice I have given previously: SAVE! SAVE! SAVE! FORFEIT ALL PLEASURES UNTIL YOU HAVE PURCHASED YOUR HOME. You have the rest of your lives to enjoy yourselves.

Reader's Notes

Reader's Notes

Reader's Notes